THE ARAB SPRING

Walt & Diane

thank you.

Lasenan Ufh, PhD

THE ARAB SPRING

MEDIATION AND PEACEFUL POLITICAL TRANSITION

LASERIAN UGOH

TATE PUBLISHING
AND ENTERPRISES, LLC

Published by Tate Publishing & Enterprises, LLC
127 E. Trade Center Terrace | Mustang, Oklahoma 73064 USA
1.888.361.9473 | www.tatepublishing.com

Tate Publishing is committed to excellence in the publishing industry. The company reflects the philosophy established by the founders, based on Psalm 68:11,
"The Lord gave the word and great was the company of those who published it."

Cover design by Joseph Emnace
Interior design by Mary Jean Archival

Published in the United States of America

ISBN: 978-1-63306-608-3
Political Science / International Relations / General
14.07.21

My mother did not take full advantage of Western education. She was a committed housewife, taking care of seven children. She and my father had an unwritten “separation of powers.” While my mother’s duty was mainly domestic affairs, my father was saddled with external matters. My father was the “minister of commerce” while my mother was the “department of treasury.” Both of them ran a happy home, raising children who are not rocket scientists or radically educated, but who find meaning and contentment in life.

If my parents ran the affairs of the Middle East, there would not have been any Arab Spring to write about. Mom would have used her soft voice to get individuals to be responsible and act responsibly for peace and harmony. This is how she is known in the little village where she unofficially mediates in communal and family matters.

Ezinne Rose, thank you for being a good mother.

ACKNOWLEDGEMENTS

I hardly thank the Head of State for being a good leader, for that is his work. It is not my thing to give praise to the office cleaner for keeping things in their proper place, it is in her job description. Yet it would not be me if I fail to express gratitude to individuals for doing extraordinary things when nobody is watching over them.

The following people have distinguished themselves in numerous ways in the completion of this work: Fr. Anthony O. Nwachukwu, Ph.D., Psy.D., Professor of Counseling Psychology and West African Studies at the Graduate Theological Foundation; Sr. (Dr.) Christiana Onyewuche, EHJ., Archdiocese of Boston. Both of them encouraged me to get into the program and supported me to the end. Thanks to Rachel Wohl, Esq., Executive Director, Maryland Mediation and Conflict Resolution Office; Dr. Michael Oladejo and Mr. Joseph Anastasio, who contributed to the data collection of this work. Thanks also to the staff of the libraries of Baltimore County and the University of Maryland for assisting me with materials and suggestions.

Like a kindergarten student who knew little or nothing of his subject, I relied heavily on the moderator of this work—Dr. Mary Kendall Hope, Professor of Mediation, Cloverdale College. I was not disappointed.

Fr. William Peterson, CSsR, has been a friend from the very day he became my tennis partner. He has not ceased to be there for me. Fr. Matt Buening, Chinwe Agbakoba, Nkeiru Mirian Nwaigwe, Chisty and Athan Nwadike have all played some role in maintaining peace and order in their various ways.

Bede, Esther, Carmina, Patrick, and Lazarus are my siblings who always pray for peace in all of human families, and in the minds and hearts of individual members of such families. The people of Ihitte-Ubi in Mbaise, Nigeria, have for many years had land disputes with their neighbors in Mbano and Ikeduru. With the power of mediation, they have coexisted all these years. I thank the impartial mediators for making peace in these villages connected only by an arable land mass.

Thanks to the Jimmy Carter Foundation for Peace. Your scholarship contribution helped when it was really needed. Many thanks to the Community Mediation Center in Baltimore, Maryland, and to the faculty of Graduate Theological Foundation in Mishawaka, Indiana.

If I write every name of persons who contributed to the success of this work, the system may be clogged. They are too numerous to mention. But the outstanding thing about it is that some of them did not even know how much their simple statements encouraged me.

CONTENTS

ABSTRACT

The Arab region with rich cultural diversity is capable of harnessing the rich potentials of its teaming youth who resort to violence due to the effect of existential vacuum and unguarded indoctrination. It was the failure of the old brigade to positively engage the people that partly gave rise to the Arab Spring. One way of unifying the populace or at least enlightening the people is to reach out to schools to incorporate diversity awareness in their curricula. It is not just enough to start early to teach children the recital of the holy books. If their knowledge of the holy books were combined with their sense of unity, the Arab world would regain its glory as the region with rich cultural and educational base. This will in turn bring about lasting peace and security as well as prosperity in the region, free of superstition. The new Arab Spring leaders must realize that truth breeds reconciliation, reconciliation gives rise to peace, a peaceful society is a happy society, and a happy society is a prosperous society.

INTRODUCTION

> He knew when to compromise. Yet he never compromised his principles. He was a militant. Yet a militant who knew how to plan, assess concrete situations, and emerge with rational solutions to problems.
>
> —Nelson Mandela

The Arab Spring, an uprising that began in Tunisia in December 2010 changed the political, religious, and cultural face of the Middle East (Blight, Pulham, & Torpey). Consequently, the following year (2011) saw a flurry of activities around North Africa and the Middle East and beyond. These activities graduated from a one-man street protest, which culminated in self-immolation of a Tunisian man to a generational upheaval, taking its toll on human and material resources. The resultant revolutionary protests and strikes snowballed into what is now a movement that is continuing to remold the societal structure of this region and the entire regions of the world.

The Arab Spring was "previously used beginning in March 2005 by numerous media commentators to suggest that a spin-off benefit of the invasion of Iraq would be the flowering of Western-friendly Middle East democracies" (Rifai 2011). If the West and the Middle East have become such sweet hearts, it is only in their hearts. The practicality of such alliance is yet to be felt in their political and bilateral relationships.

Various interest groups and individuals have tried to formulate titles for the situation in the region. Some of those titles include the following: Arab Awakening, Arab upheaval, Arab revolution, Arab conflict, Arab uprising. Of all the titles, one thing is common—it is regional. Little wonder why one of those interest individuals remarks thus:

> I prefer to call it the Arab upheaval or the Arab uprising. The reason for that is that it is genuinely Arab. It's not something that's happening country by country. It's happening across the entire region simultaneously, with everybody really intensely conscious of the regional nature of it.
>
> —Lynch 2012

From my personal analogy, the term, Arab Spring, is so common because most of the protests targeting Arab despotic rulers took place or started around and about spring. Since after winter comes spring, this concept also alludes to the fact that weeding out corrupt despots is likened to shedding of leaves in winter, followed by springing of new leaves; meaning the rise of new leaderships. If the name were *Arab Hurricane*, it would possibly be so violent that no new leaders would survive in such environment. But the idea is not to eliminate all forms of leadership, for a society without a meaningful leadership is bound to fail. It was rather an effort aimed to eliminate despotic leaders and supplant them with more malleable and people-friendly ones.

The emotions that motivated the people to create this revolution against the oppressive tyrannies reflect the same force of conflict resolution that drives the goals of mediation. For to stand up and expect to be heard equally and respected accordingly, is the main ingredient in successful resolution of disputes. Mediation in the Middle East must, therefore, take cognizance of the fact that the various parties to the Arab Spring must freely express themselves so that lasting peace could hold sway in the region and beyond.

This study is aimed at an in-depth analysis of the revolution, otherwise known as the Arab Spring. The main characters in the theater, mainly the deposed leaders and their antagonists, have contributed in the events leading to rewriting of human history. One question, which seeks sincere and conscientious response, remains whether the international community would have done anything differently to produce a different result. Some interest groups have blamed the international community for undue delays in responding to conflicts in the Middle East. Others have accused Western countries of complicity in the Arab revolution. Who is right and wrong is not part of the discussions in this work. However, a look at the appropriateness or otherwise of interventions of the Western world in the Arab conflicts will feature prominently herein.

Since its inception following the events of the Second World War, the United Nations has played vital mediation roles across the globe. Some of these mediation efforts have been so successful that issues were resolved for good. Some have not been so successful because of various reasons, ranging from the nature of the issues to the personality of the mediators and to the mediation techniques. Could the world body's mediation have made the outcome of the Arab Spring and the lives of the people any better? Does international mediation really matter in the face of crises? Did the leaders of the various countries ignore signs of the impending crises and the possibility of employing experienced experts in mediation to try defusing tensions prior to the Arab Spring? These are some of the relevant questions which will be addressed in the course of this work.

Specifically, the use of mediation in conflict resolution will be one central focus of this work. This entire discourse is intended to reveal ways that a more peaceful transition stands a better chance of happening if proper mediation techniques and skilled mediators are engaged in conflict resolutions. These trained mediators must be vast in specific international mediation skill, with specific regard to the languages of those involved, and the historical and most salient cultural factors that influence the leadership decisions.

While the study is not an attempt at exhaustively providing a full history of the Arab world conflicts, it will study certain origins of conflicts in the region. The intention here is far from making this a panacea or silver bullet for settling conflicts all over the globe. Nonetheless, this study will touch on the role of mediation in addressing issues before they escalate. Even after a conflict, there is hope for reconciliation, which is made possible by proper mediation techniques. Although it is not a study of leadership, it will discuss issues bordering on possession of power and authority. Certain notable leadership figures will be presented and discussed in relation to their styles and contributions to world history and human relations.

Arab Spring, for the purpose of this work, will not be limited to the revolutionary events of winter 2010 in Tunisia to Summer 2011 in Libya, involving a vendor in Tunisia and a head of state in Libya. The study will date back to pre-independence years of certain countries of the region as well as of some sub-Sahara African countries. Past and recent efforts by the international community aimed at peaceful mediation around the region will also come into focus.

ANTECEDENTS OF THE ARAB SPRING

From Harry Truman (1945) to George W. Bush (2001), virtually every American president has tried to mediate in conflicts in the Arab world. Many of these mediation efforts have produced positive results. The problem is that the resultant reprieves are often short-lived. It's not been a happy history (Tristam 2012, 1). Some of the resolutions last as long as the meeting ends and the negotiators return to their constituents. The intent to satisfy the people sometimes is the reason these accords are so short-lived. While the negotiators believe they have reached a consensus, their constituents may not be satisfied with such agreements. This has caused the death of leaders in the past. Anwar el Sadat of Egypt was one such victim.

> On Oct. 6, 1981, while celebrating the eight anniversary of the 1973 war against Israel. Sadat was gunned down during the military parade. His assailants had been members of a Muslim Brotherhood breakaway group who declared him an apostate (for not imposing

> Sharia law in Egypt) and denounced the peace treaty with Israel.
>
> —Tristam 2012

The purpose of mediation is "bringing people together with an unbiased third party in order to settle a dispute" (Schechter 2012, 1). Since mediation is aimed at attaining this purpose, some individuals and groups are yet to get the message right. An example is this statement credited to an influential public opinion analyst. "But we do live in a world where we can take actions in pursuit of policies that serve our national interests. For example, it would be in our interest to weaken ties between Syria and Iran" (Johnson 2011, 1).

As if in concert with the above writer, former United States president G. W. Bush, commenting on the interventions in the Middle East, remarked, "And if the United States tires of fighting in the streets of Baghdad,...we will face the terrorists in the streets of our own cities...So the United States will not leave until victory is achieved..." (Stout 2006, 1). Is the aim to achieve victory against the enemy or to work towards peace in a conflict-ridden region of the world?

In mediation, the disputants take the center stage and decide their own fate. The best resolution to a crisis is usually formulated and implemented by the disputants themselves. "The mediator's role is to facilitate communication between the parties, not to impose solutions. Mediators do not advise, take sides or render a judgment. Instead, the mediator will work with all the parties to help them reach a mutually acceptable resolution" (Ccrchicago.org 2012).

This work will take another look at the Middle East conflicts, with a view to address those areas where the international community needs to address the region's issues.

Previous approaches have often succeeded in selling a tailor-made idea of conflict resolution to an entirely different culture. I believe that the people of the region would be happy to live in peace and harmony. So far, the Arab people have been confused with a style of mediation that is *forced* on them from the West. Therefore, we need to present options for methods of mediation that have been successful in this region, which may serve to assist the new leadership of the Arab Spring to begin a new way of resolving their conflicts.

THE ARAB SPRING

The Arab Spring has enjoyed popular acceptance and support from numerous progressive groups and individuals. However, not everyone is on board in matters relating to the situation in the Middle East. One such seeming dissenting voice was that of a former worker with the Central Intelligence Agency and United States State Department's Office of Counter Terrorism who remarks:

> Hosni Mubarak was not a thug…he was a cooperating partner with the United States in helping secure the border of Israel and pursuing a peace agreement with Israel…Furthermore he was in the forefront of battling Islamic extremists in Egypt…When the protests broke out in Cairo he had every right to expect the United States to have his back. We bolted and abandoned him. And this has set off a chain reaction. Despots and strongmen in Saudi Arabia, Yemen and Bahrain now find themselves no longer able to rely on the United States. So it should not come as a surprise that these folks start pursuing their own survival…
>
> —Johnson 2012, 1

From the foregoing, it is indicative that "to have his back" in this context may have meant to mediate in the conflict. Similarly, "pursuing their own survival" likely meant to fight back. This points to the fact that an early and timely mediation would have saved some, if not all, of these precarious situations in the Arab world. An example is the situation in Syria. "And the more the outside world sits idly by as Syrians are slaughtered, the more the Sunnis in Syria will believe that the world turns a blind eye to such horrors because of their religion" (Cagaptay 2012, 1).

The whole attempt at formulating a title for the conflicts in the Arab region has captured a lot of attention. Numerous authors have suggested titles and argued against other writers' suggestions. One such argument goes thus:

> Springtime has always been associated with renewal, so perhaps it was inevitable that the Arab uprisings would earn the title "Arab Spring." Considering the track record of that Arab spring, why would anyone want to burden the Arab uprisings with this title? And there are two other reasons to discourage its use. First, the term spring implies a positive outcome for the uprisings, which has yet to be achieved. Second, only one of the uprisings—Syria—actually broke out in that season (if one includes all of March in spring). The others began in the dead of winter, a season hardly appropriate for an uplifting title.
>
> —Gelvin 2012, 33

Arab Spring was, and continues to be, debated as the title of this movement. The description of this movement is continuing to evolve—it may best be defined with the inclusion of appropriate mediation techniques—that would enhance its ability to stimulate positive growth, as opposed to negative perpetuation of conflict.

On the genesis of the Arab Spring, various opinions have been advanced. One popular one is that the revolt was a result of a despairing Tunisian fruit vendor named Mohamed Bouazizi *who* took one way out, setting himself on fire to protest the injustices of the status quo. "THE REVOLT was a settlement of accounts between the powers that be and populations determined to be done with despots" (Fouad 2012, 1).

MEDIATION

George and Jane were married for the past ten years and had no offspring. They blamed each other for the barrenness. It came to a point that they refused to talk to each other. Their friends and relatives offered to mediate in their feud and were refused. So they lived in the same room not speaking to one another.

One morning, George had an appointment for a job interview. Since he had not had a job for months, he believed that was the main reason for the fight in the house. He therefore thought that the new job would be that magic wand to settle their domestic problem. The only huddle was how to wake up early enough to keep the appointment. He had no alarm clock, and as a heavy sleeper, he needed someone to wake him up early to make it to the bus stop.

Since he and Jane were the only ones in the house and were not on talking terms, he had difficulty communicating his request to his wife. Later in the middle of the night, he decided to pull a fast one. He wrote a note on a piece of paper and placed it on Jane's side of the bed. The note read: "please wake me up at five o'clock." When Jane woke up and saw the note, she replied on the flip side of the same note: "please, it is five o'clock, wake up," and placed it on the sleepy George. Of course, George did not see the note until he woke at about seven o'clock.

At that moment, George needed no diviner to tell him that his prospect for a job had become a tall dream. It was indeed the anticlimax of a ten-year-old marriage. George and Jane gave room to an acrimonious relationship, which caused him a job as well as their marriage. Only if humility had prevailed, they would have welcomed mediators when the problem started brewing.

It is interesting to note that mediation has been in existence from the first day people started having misunderstanding. It originally started in association with the court system, meaning that one had to be in the legal profession to mediate. "Today, however, interest in mediation is slowly developing in the cognate fields of psychology, sociology, social work, pastoral counseling, and pastoral psychology" (Chan 2007, 5).

Citing Leviton and Greenstone, Henry Chan—in his book *The Humanity of Mediators* (2007)—defines mediation as "the intervention of a neutral third party, who intervening at the request of the parties assists the parties at dispute in finding their own way out of the dispute through equity through consensus" (2007, 7). Chan goes further to cite other notable names in the field of mediation. Jennifer Beer with Eileen Stief, according to Chan, defines mediation as "any process for resolving disputes in which another person helps the parties negotiate a settlement" (2007, 7).

In his summation, Chan infers that "mediation is a process which involves three parties—a neutral third party and the two disputants who work towards the goal of reaching an agreement or a consensus" (2007, 8). He therefore propounds thirteen "assumptions" including, but not limited to the following:

1. Mediation assumes that people can resolve conflicts and are capable of discovering their own resources for doing so.
2. Mediators define and control the structure of the process but seldom make suggestions or give advice.
3. Disputants control the content of conflict issues and make the decision.
4. Values, beliefs and attitudes are not the focus of mediation but can be discussed and may be useful in clarifying issues for both parties.
5. Participants in a mediation are likely to carry out agreements because they are personally involved in making the decision and have a stake in the outcome.

In addition, it is noteworthy that "mediation assumes that the disputants have a desire and are willing to work within the process toward an amicable and mutual agreement or resolution" (Chan 2007, 10).

In the same vein, there are circumstances when it would be imprudent to pursue mediation. Citing Beer and Stief, Chan enumerated those circumstances, including but not limited to the following:

> 1. A serious incident has just occurred and people are still too upset to carry on a useful conversation.
> 2. One party seems incapable of listening to anything you say, or seems otherwise too disturbed to negotiate a workable agreement.

3. You believe that one party might be better off using the courts or other forum. Power imbalance makes fair agreement unlikely.
4. Key parties are unwilling to participate.

2007, 10

Mediation is a serious business as well as a sensitive one. Therefore, if the setting is wrongly chosen and/or arranged, the outcome might be regrettable. In light of this, certain experts in mediation have adduced various aspects to consider in arranging for mediation. Some of the popular opinions include the fact that "the physical setting can have an impact on facilitating communication, gaining control of the argument, reducing or increasing pressure on the parties, and insuring the safety of all those involved" (Chan, Leviton, Greenstone).

Mediation experts emphasize the need to select a neutral venue for mediation. The reasoning here is "that the disputants must feel equally empowered" (2007, 11).

Regarding the choice of site, some factors must be put into consideration, such as

1. privacy,
2. sufficient lighting,
3. absence of distraction,
4. adequate space/ventilation,
5. adequate security, and
6. easy accessibility.

2007, 12

The general rules for mediation setting in the words of Jennifer E. Beer with Eileen Steief (1997) are the following:

> 1. Everyone should be able to see and hear everyone else and participate easily in discussions.
> 2. Members of one party should be able to sit together if they choose. Couples typically want to sit side by side.
> 3. Everyone should be physically comfortable, undistracted, and feel as safe as possible.
> 4. The mediators should be able to control the process.
> 5. The setting should suggest mediator impartiality.
> 6. Pick a location that feels comfortable and private: not too large, not too dim or cluttered.
>
> 1997, 28

The suitable furniture for mediation is a round table or a square table, or a rectangular table. The sitting arrangement is strictly important.

> Appropriate mediators should possess intelligence, tact, drafting skills, a sense of humor, and have specific knowledge and expertise of the conflict at hand. Mediators who possess these attributes are likely to be acceptable to all sides in a conflict, and consequently enhance the parties' motivation to reach a peaceful settlement.
>
> —Bercovitch 2003, 20

Corroborating Bercovitch, Chan notes: "the mediator is expected to be a neutral third party" (2007, 14). Citing Beer with Stief, Chan identifies some personality traits and skills of a good mediator:

> 1. Strong "people skills, especially giving good attention.
> 2. Able to be directive and to confront.

3. Comfortable with high emotions, arguments, interruptions, tears.
4. Respected and trusted.
5. Imaginative in solving problems.
6. Patient as disputants inch their way towards resolution.
7. Able to empathize and be gentle, to withhold judgment.
8. Impartial: putting aside one's own opinions, reactions, and even some principles.
9. Low need for recognition, credit, having things turn out your way.

2007, 14

The talent is reflected in the sensitivity with which the mediator listens, hears, responds, empathizes, creates, draws parties into the process, and deftly maneuvers through the delicate and difficult moments with an intuitive sense of timing and appropriateness (Chan, Leviton, Greenstone).

In my estimation, many prominent names in the field of mediation are of one opinion. Henry Chan, Jacob Bercovitck, Jennifer Beer with Eileen Steif, Sharon Leviton and James Greenstone. All agree that the mediation process is a serious business, which requires the commitment of seasoned mediators possessing those qualities as enumerated above.

MEDIATION PROCESS

The mediation process consists of four different stages, namely: i) Opening Statement, ii) Information Sharing and Issue Identification, iii) Exchange and Negotiation, iv) Agreement and Conclusion.

These four stages are discussed in details below:

1. Opening Statement.

   At this stage, Chan cites Myers and Filner assigning roles to the mediator and the co-mediator. According to Chan, "The mediator discusses the process, and describes the mediator's role, the roles of the participants, and the general expectations for the mediation" (Chan 2007, 17).

   Quoting Leviton and Greenstone, Chan gives the purposes of the Opening Statement as summarized below:

   - Establish a safe environment to negotiate.
   - Establish the mediator's credibility and control of the proceedings.
   - Explain the mediation process and what will be asked of the parties.
   - Obtain necessary commitments from the parties concerning their involvement.
   - Be sensitive to concerns raised by the parties.

   2007, 18

   Before the actual commencement of mediation, the mediator must assure the disputants of his/her neutrality. The disputants must make a commitment to respect each other's time and values. "Expectations are also pointed out to the parties in regard to their commitment to the time required for resolving the issues, after which they are requested to provide their consent to commence the process." (2007, 19).

2. Information Sharing and Issue Identification

   This stage involves data gathering. According to Chan, Leviton and Greenstone provide a concrete approach, thus:

- Ask each disputant to state his/her perception of the conflict. Hear all evidence pertinent to the dispute. Collect any evidence relating to the dispute, such as written contracts, cancelled checks, receipts, and reports.
- Clarify issues.
- Clarify remaining differences and see whether the disputants can form a common understanding.
- Listen actively to the disputants' issues and feelings as they are talking.

2007, 19

Still in this stage, Chan mentions Leviton and Greenstone as proposing "guidelines for the mediator in respect to the information that is provided as follows":

- Learn about the parties' interests and priorities.
- Determine whether the parties agree on the credibility of the incidents and information.
- Clarify the differences and see whether the parties can form a common understanding.
- Formulate clear goals.
- Attempt to settle simple issues. Build on success.
- Note parties' underlying needs and hopes. These are at the core of the dispute. Having them addressed and met will be the core of a resolution.

2007, 20–21

3. Exchange and Negotiation.

"During this stage," according to Chan, "the disputants must take an active role and directly communicate their needs and interests." He also cited Leviton and Greenstone as inferring that "this will create the psychological ownership that will make the final agreement work" (2007, 21).

It is understood that the third stage encompasses problem solving, but not limited to it. Beer with Stief is quoted as concluding that "The Building the Agreement phase is the time for parties to

- identify and evaluate a range of ideas,
- negotiate with everyone's interests in mind,
- develop and test specific proposals, and
- Gain confidence in their ability to resolve the situation and to build commitment to the emerging agreement.

2007, 22

4. Agreement and Conclusion

   An agreement between disputants "will contain all the statements that they have arrived at through a meeting of the minds" (2007, 22).

   Chan writes that Beer and Stief identify elements that an agreement should contain, namely

- details specifics: who, what, when;
- is evenhanded and not conditional;
- uses clear, familiar wording;
- emphasizes positive action;
- deals with any pending proceedings; and
- provides for the future.

2007, 22–23

MEDIATOR STYLES

The four mediator styles are as listed below, namely

1. Facilitative Mediation,
2. Transformative Mediation,

3. Evaluative Mediation, and
4. Restorative Justice Mediation.

The first three were the original styles of mediation. Later, Restorative Justice became part of the group.

RESTORATIVE JUSTICE MEDIATION

Although last in the group, it is described as "a systematic response to wrongdoing that emphasizes healing the wounds of victims, offenders and communities caused or revealed by the criminal behavior" (*Mediation and Conflict Resolution Office* 1999, 1).

The main point in Restorative Justice Mediation is "identifying and taking steps to repair harm" (Chan 2007, 29). Another focal point here is to identify the nature and extent of the victim's loss and to explore how the offender might begin to repair the harm caused by the criminal act. Yet another important aspect is that "agreements are made concerning restitution schedules, follow-up meetings and monitoring procedures" (Chan, Van Ness, and Strong).

FACILITATIVE MEDIATION

This is said to be the foremost style of mediation. Citing Zumeta, Chan notes that in facilitative mediation, "the mediator structures a process to assist the parties in reaching a mutually agreeable resolution" (2007, 25).

One advantage of this style is that it empower(s) parties, and help the parties take responsibility for their own disputes and the resolution of the disputes. The flip side of this style is that mediation takes too long, and too often ends without agreement (Zumeta 2011, 1).

TRANSFORMATIVE MEDIATION

Chan quoting Brad Spangler in a summary of a list of ten distinctive points, written by Robert A. Baruch Bush and Joseph P. Folger, enumerates the points, which I succinctly list, thus:

> 1. Transformative mediators leave responsibility for the outcomes with the parties.
> 2. Transformative mediators feel (and express) a sense of success when empowerment and recognition occur, even in small degrees. They do not see a lack of settlement as a failure.
>
> 2007, 27

Tramsformative mediation has similar advantages and disadvantages as facilitative mediation. In addition, Zina notes that supporters of transformative mediation "worry that outcomes can be contrary to standards of fairness and that mediators in these approaches cannot protect the weaker party" (Zumeta 2011, 1).

EVALUATIVE MEDIATION

According to Zumeta in evaluative mediation, the "mediator structures the process, and directly influences the outcome of mediation" (2011, 1). The kernel of this approach, therefore, is summarized in these words:

> In evaluative mediation, the mediator controls the process and suggests solutions for resolving the conflict. The focus of an evaluative mediation is primarily upon settlement. The mediators will make

> their best efforts to get the parties to compromise, if necessary, to achieve a result.
>
> —Mediation and Conflict Resolution Office

Of the four mediation styles, Facilitative Mediation is my preferred choice of mediation style. I would choose this style over and above the other styles for the following reason: "the mediator structures a process to assist the parties in reaching a mutually agreeable resolution" (Zumeta 2000, 1). One advantage of this style is that it "empower[s] parties, and help the parties take responsibility for their own disputes and the resolution of the disputes" (2000, 1). The flip side of this style is that "mediation takes too long, and too often ends without agreement" (2000, 1).

FACTORS INFLUENCING MEDIATION

MEDIATION AND CULTURE

The Arab Spring breeze blew through the several regions of the world, encompassing several peoples and cultures. Therefore, any discussion on Arab Spring must take into account the various cultural sensibilities of the regions of the world. To mediate in issues bothering on the Arab Spring, therefore, the professional mediator must be culturally diverse. In this section, I will define culture and its relationship with mediation.

Culture is a representation of the customary beliefs, social forms, and material traits of a racial, religious, or social group; *also*: the characteristic features of everyday existence (as diversions or a way of life) shared by people in a place or time…" (*The Free Merriam-Webster Dictionary*).

An English Anthropologist defines culture as "that complex whole which includes knowledge, belief, art, law, morals, custom, and any other capabilities and habits acquired by man as a member of society" (Tylor 1871, 1).

> *Culture* refers to the following Ways of Life, including but not limited to:
>
> 1. *Language*: the oldest human institution and the most sophisticated medium of expression.
> 2. *Arts & Sciences*: the most advanced and refined forms of human expression.
> 3. *Thought*: the ways in which people perceive, interpret, and understand the world around them.
> 4. *Spirituality*: the value system transmitted through generations for the inner well-being of human beings, expressed through language and actions.
> 5. *Social activity*: the shared pursuits within a cultural community, demonstrated in a variety of festivities and life-celebrating events.
> 6. *Interaction*: the social aspects of human contact, including the give-and-take of socialization, negotiation, protocol, and conventions.
>
> —Roshan Cultural Heritage Institute 2001

It is often the case that cultural differences constitute the most common cause of misunderstanding between parties in dispute as well as between disputants and the mediator. In international mediation, some of the cultural differences might be religious, language, demeanor, etcetera. The challenging question then is how a mediator remains neutral and objective in the event that his/her cultural identity and philosophy differ from those of the disputants.

Familiarity with the disputants' culture is one way a mediator wins the trust of the disputants. As a mediator who finds himself mediating in a culture other than his, he should first of all get to understand the people's culture by educating himself. Education in this regard is to ask questions from locals who are not directly connected to the dispute. He should also spend time in the given environment, with a view to understanding how the people relate with people who do not belong to their cultural group. He should read books on the people's cultural norms.

In the event that I get the opportunity to mediate in a dispute between people whose cultural norms differ from mine, my attitude to them would be that of empathy as opposed to a judgmental stance. If, for instance, I am mediating in a Muslim culture, I would probably start each session with a prayer led by one of the disputants in their own religious tradition. If they were not keen in starting with a prayer, I would let them understand that it is all about them and their intention to settle their dispute, however they arrive at such settlement.

As a mediator in a Muslim community, which requires that women cover their head in public occasions, I would suggest that any female co-mediator identifies with their dress code without losing her identity. If the dispute were not religious in nature, I would endeavor to avoid any religious trappings as we direct all resources to the subject matter. If my appearance would make them feel more at ease with me, I would try to adorn flowing gowns and wear a goatee like the rest of them, without deviating from my mission.

An average Muslim feels that women's place in society is mainly consultative in domestic affairs. Some Muslims believe that women should be seen and not heard. So when the United States Department sends women as emissaries to the Middle East, some Muslims see it as a matter of insensitivity on the part of the United States.

In terms of the emissaries and diplomats to the region, they should identify with the culture of the people and dress appropriately. If the secretary of state were to meet with the

Emir of Baghdad (as an example), though she is American and represents American interest, dressing like an average Iraqi woman for just that purpose would not make her less of a secretary of state or less of an American.

Dressing like the people is a way of identifying with them. By identifying with them, there is less tension and suspicion by the people. This is where relationships begin to heal, and the people begin to develop trust in the American mission in the region.

Finally, I would try to see their points of view as influenced by their environment. I would carefully and patiently listen to them in an effort to find a common ground toward the resolution of their dispute. This becomes important because cultural differences could be such a sensitive issue that might be misconstrued if not handled properly. In an international mediation, culture could make or mar a negotiation.

For a mediator who finds himself/herself in a culture other than his/her cultural circle, it takes more than education to fit into the group. It takes tact, sensitivity, intelligence, tolerance, and discipline to mediate in such environment. Such cross-cultural mediation is not as easy as it seems. It is only when the disputants trust the mediator and the mediator empathizes with the disputants that the hope of a successful mediation is possible.

When a mediator appreciates the importance of Cultural Empathy, mediation is half attained. Empathy, in this context, is defined as intellectual and emotional awareness and understanding of another person's thoughts, feelings, and behavior even that are distressing. It emphasizes understanding. When a mediator empathizes with disputants, the mediator creates a safe and balanced environment in which people can be heard as they wish to be heard (faculty.mc3.edu, Empatia Resolutions).

MEDIATION AND LANGUAGE

Language is often the first barrier and at the very least an ongoing challenge to any international mediation. The problem of language is more intense when the disputants and the mediator come from different language groups, as is the case in many international mediations, including mediating in the Arab world. Granted, the problem of language could be addressed by the use of an interpreter or translator, which is not without its own tension.

Language is a vital element in mediation. As a vital element, it has to be spoken and understood for it to achieve its intended outcome. If, for instance, I have the opportunity to mediate in a conflict between Israel and Palestine, I would do a couple of things. Since I do not understand or speak neither Hebrew nor Arabic, there has to be a common front, in the form of forging an alliance with both sides by researching some common words and phrases to all three languages. Again, if the Israeli and the Palestinian negotiators do not understand each other's language nor do they speak nor understand the mediator's language, I would be compelled to employ the services of a couple of interpreters or translators.

In order to engage the right interpreter or translator, I must make sure that the interpreter or translator understands the whole purpose of the mediation. I would make sure that the interpreter/translator is transparent and neutral and is not in any way sympathetic to either of the disputant's cause. I would ask questions regarding his opinion about the Jewish occupation of Gaza and West Bank. I would ask his/her take on the independence of Palestine as a sovereign state. A denial or affirmation of the occupation, or a biased opinion over the Palestinian sovereignty would indicate subjectivity and a possible prejudgment.

I would simply remind him/her that the job of the interpreter is limited to being a liaison between the mediator and the disputants, and that his/her personal opinions are not welcome.

Disputants want to know the credibility, integrity, intelligence, knowledge, and familiarity of the subject matter by the mediator in any given situation. In light of this situation, I would reassure the disputants that I am seasoned in my profession. I would make reference to my previous accomplishments and mediation successes in the past. I would proudly inform them that I was a product of adroit professors of the Graduate Theological Foundation. I would emphasize my neutrality and transparency. I would indicate my willingness to learn some rudiments of the languages. I would assure them of my familiarity with the history and culture of the Middle East and the attendant religious, cultural, and territorial disputes dating back to the ancient days. I would reassure them that I have come with an approach aimed at brokering a lasting peaceful coexistence and tranquility to a people who have seem all sorts of disruption to normal living. I would exhibit my unbiased and genuine interest in their cause.

Finally, I would be mindful of expert opinions, which stipulate that appropriate mediators should possess intelligence, tact, drafting skills, a sense of humor, and have specific knowledge and expertise of the conflict at hand. Mediators who possess these attributes are likely to be acceptable to all sides in a conflict, and consequently enhance the parties' motivation to reach a peaceful settlement (Bercovitch 2003, 20).

In summary, language barrier could make or mar a mediation process the same way the use of translators is vital to the success or failure of a mediation setting.

MEDIATION AND POWER BALANCE

According to Dr. Hope, in mediation, *power* is the careful consideration of who is being perceived as important or *powerful* in the mediation at any given time. She, therefore, infers that, *keeping the power balanced* in mediation refers to the efforts made by the mediation through specific techniques to assure that each separate disputant is being equally heard and thereby given equal significance and equal respect and consideration for his or her perspective (Hope 2010).

POWER BALANCE BETWEEN DISPUTANTS

Power balance enables disputants to present their issues on an equal basis. It facilitates an unbiased resolution of disputes by the parties involved in negotiation. Bercovitch (2003) citing Young notes: "the smaller the power difference between the two parties, the more successful will be the mediator" (2003, 37).

WHY POWER BALANCE?

Power balance is important because when disputants negotiate as equals, there is the plausibility of a successful resolution of dispute. It is also the case that "When disputants feel equally respected and that each have an equally important perspective they are free to let go of anger and their singular position. It frees them to consider the other side's perspective and consider how the other side may have valid and important perspectives also" (Hope 2010). Again, where there is a power balance, none of the disputing parties will feel left out of the reconciliation process.

Where there is a power balance, the outcome of negotiation is often acceptable by the parties. Such agreements as reached in a power-balanced negotiation results from a relaxed atmosphere conducive for free expression and presentation of various sides to the case. As a result, individuals stand a better chance of accepting such agreements as binding and possibly lasting.

MEDIATOR'S POWER BALANCE BETWEEN DISPUTANTS

A good mediator usually allots equal and same amount of time to all disputants to express their concern and their own side of the story. He/she maintains a safe environment for both parties. He/she maintains some noticeable measure of neutrality in the course of mediation.

POWER BALANCE CRUCIAL TO INSURING A LASTING POSITIVE CHANGE

When disputants negotiate as equals, they freely express their frustration. This freedom of expression gives rise to an amicable, unrestrained and possible lasting resolution of the conflict.

Where a negotiator suspects an imbalance in negotiation power between disputants, he must tactically ensure a balance without compromising his neutrality. To buttress this point, it is noted thus: "…the mediator's obligation with regard to negotiation power is to ensure that each party in mediation has sufficient capacity to effectively represent their interests in mediation" (Oregon Mediation Center, Inc.).

PERCEPTION OF THE DISPUTANTS OF THE MEDIATOR'S STATUS OF POWER AS COMPARED TO THEIR OWN

The perception of the disputants of the mediator's status of power is highly important. According to Bercovitch (2003), some mediators are better able to marshal resources, be more persuasive. They possess leverage and can use social influence that could be crucial in persuading the parties to make concessions or move toward an agreement. (2003, 20). In the same vein, if the disputants don't respect the mediator as *valid* or a powerful enough figure—they will not engage in mediation (Hope 2010).

Perception of power is as important as possession of actual power in negotiation. Nonetheless, perception is never the same as reality. Perception is what a person makes of reality. The relationship between perception of power and power is as expressed by Ury, et al.

> If you conclude (perceive) that you are more powerful, you may relax and not prepare as well as you should. On the other hand, if you conclude (perceive) that you are weaker than the other side, there is a risk that you will be discouraged and again not devote sufficient attention to how you might persuade them.
>
> 1991, 178

Perception of power, therefore, could be described as a double-edged sword, which if handled properly, could be a veritable tool; otherwise could cause irreparable harm either way.

PERCEPTION OF EQUAL GROUND AND POWER WITH DISPUTANTS AND MEDIATOR

As a mediator, I can assist the disputant to perceive that I am on equal ground and power with him/her by doing a number of things. Since it is an established fact that a successful mediation depends on the disputants' ability to establish unalloyed trust and confidence in the mediator and the entire process, I will assure the disputant that I am familiar with their situation. I will let them understand that I am only a neutral mediator, with no vested interest in either of the parties. I will let them understand that my mediation depends on their willingness to resolve their dispute, and that I am only an instrument (facilitator) to the process.

In order to keep the perception of equal power present, the following steps are helpful:

I will let disputants understand that there is power in developing a good working relationship between each other. I will suggest that they seek power in understanding their interests. I will call their attention to the fact that to invent an elegant option is one important asset in negotiation. Using external standards of legitimacy is one source of power in negotiation. Disputants should, therefore, be helped to explore it. I will inform them that developing a good BATNA (Better Alternative to a Negotiated Agreement) is an important ingredient of empowerment in negotiation.

CAN MEDIATION OF A CONFLICT MAKE THE SITUATION WORSE?

Mediation can always make a conflict worse, and mediation often makes conflicts worse (Hope 2009; 2010). If the disputants notice even the slightest form of bias and prejudice by the mediator, anger might flare and the situation becomes worse than it was found. If the mediator exhibits ignorance and lack of proper knowledge of the bone of contention, he/she loses the ability to keep the situation under control. A mediator's arrogance and lack of respect for the people's cultural sensitivity could constitute a ground for an escalation of conflict.

> Sometimes, the disputants themselves are just not ready for the emotions that mediations bring up, and the mere fact that each shows up and see one another in mediation will make the conflict worse – because they say and do things there that may worsen the conflict.
>
> —Hope 2010

AN EXAMPLE OF A SITUATION IN WHICH A POWER IMBALANCE LED TO A WORSENING OF THE CONFLICT OR LED TO THE CONFLICT BECOMING WORSE

The Argentine-British dispute over the Falkland Islands is a typical example of a power imbalance leading to a worsening of the conflict. Alexander Haig, who was mediating on behalf of the United States in the dispute, proffered conditions which turned out to be a clear case of power imbalance. According to Bercovitch, (2003) "...Haig's effort to impose a solution heavily biased towards one of the disputants, forced Argentina into an underdog position it was unwilling to accept" (2003,136). Of course, the resultant effect was that the British-Argentine struggle over the Falkland Islands snowballed into a crisis of international magnitude.

HOW POLITICAL LEADERS WHO ARE "NOT" INVOLVED IN THE MEDIATION AFFECT THE MEDIATION

Political leaders possess certain leverage, combined with *carrot and stick*, which they wield through their representatives. Government sponsored mediators are often influenced by political leaders, who sometimes have ulterior motives. Again, rich political leaders make bogus financial promises to entice less privileged disputants to settle for less. Often the difficulty encountered by a mediator lies not with the negotiators but with their constituents, up the communication chain, who seem unsupportive of the negotiations or are unwilling to make the concessions deemed necessary by the mediator (Bercovitch 2003, 47).

It is imperative to note that the two political leaders must be supportive of mediation because if either is not supportive—then the mediation will be in danger of being compromised and the conflict could easily worsen to a crisis stage (Hope 2010).

IF SOMETHING GOES WRONG IN A MEDIATION

If, in the course of mediation, the parties become intolerant of each other, I will arrange to meet with each of them separately—this is often considered the last resort. If one party feels that the other is getting more attention, I will reiterate my principle of neutrality, which means fairness to both sides. If the problem is environmental, I will consider a shift of venue. "A neutral and pleasing location should be carefully selected to begin with to avoid simple environmental conflicts" (Hope 2010).

WHEN A MEDIATION IS GOING WELL

One indicator that mediation is going well is when disputants are able to present their concerns in a less acrimonious manner. Another good sign is when they are willing to listen to one another, with a view to reach a balanced settlement. Yet another sign is when they develop a cordial and mutual relationship with the mediator.

WHAT DO YOU DO WHEN A CONFLICT IS ESCALATING

When disputants express frustration and discontentment at the direction of a mediation process, it is a clear sign that a conflict is escalating. At this juncture, a good mediator needs to re-strategize and effectively change the course of mediation. The failure of disputants to continue with any form of negotiation is indicative of an escalation of conflict. A good course of action here is to reach out to the chief antagonists in the conflict.

MEDIATION TECHNIQUES

Mediation is a systematic discipline with its own language and procedure. It is only when these forms are observed that a meaningful and successful mediation is achievable. In this regard, it is extremely important that anyone aspiring to mediate in the Middle East needs to be acquainted with these techniques.

GOING TO THE BALCONY

William Ury defines the "balcony" as "a metaphor for a mental attitude of detachment. Going to the balcony means distancing yourself from your natural impulses and emotions." From the balcony you can calmly evaluate the conflict, almost as if you were a third party. You can think constructively for both sides and look for a mutually satisfactory way to resolve the problem (Ury 1991, 17).

When a five-year-old throws a tantrum, he gets *a time-out*; when the five-year-old spirit inside a full-grown man manifests in an argument, he *goes to the balcony*. Going to the balcony in this context means taking a break to reflect on the preceding event. Such temporary retreat is a time to evaluate the situation before making a commitment or taking a major decision.

Eddy and his father got into an argument regarding when to return home at night. Eddy's father had repeatedly warned him over the danger of coming home past 6.00 p.m. Eddy always gives the excuse that he works late. At sixteen years, he is not expected to be working that late, said his father. Since his family is not capable of supporting him financially, he works to take care of some minor bills. His father understands all this fact, but is still concerned about his safety in a rough neighborhood.

One evening, Eddy came home with a black eye. This was the opportunity his father was waiting for. His father cashed in on this opportunity to hold a meeting. The meeting was so heated that father and son stopped short at getting physical. Eddy vowed not to give up his job. Father offers a stern warning that Eddy must leave the house. Eddy had just started packing his few belongings when his father walked out of the room.

His father stayed in the bedroom for about ten minutes. When he remerged, Eddy was expecting another round of yelling and marching orders. Instead, his father stretched out both his arms, invited Eddy to a warm embrace. At first, Eddy was reluctant to respond because he did not know what suddenly became of his father. With hands outstretched still, his father walked up to Eddy who was busily packing up to leave, held him as both embraced each other and shed tears like little babies.

Eddy's father muttered: "I am only worried that you might be hurt, I did not mean to be hard on you." Eddy promised to discuss a change of work schedule with his supervisor.

What transpired in the above example is a case of "going to the balcony" to find a solution to an argument. Eddy stock to his position of keeping his job. His father maintained his interest in the safety of his son. Since both were reluctant to budge, his father finally took a time-out, stepped aside for ten minutes. This was an opportunity for father and son to douse their tension and came to an agreement.

Going to the balcony is in no way punitive. If anything, it is highly recommended that people take a break, "spread their wings," count to ten, inhale and exhale deeply to clear their brain and mind before making a clear, conscious, non-coerced, free commitment.

STEP TO THEIR SIDE AND REFRAME

There is a wise saying that "When a conscienceless power meets a powerless conscience, the former laughs first, and the latter laughs last". Of course, it is a known fact that he who laughs last laughs best. The Scriptures have it that if your adversary demands that you walk one mile, prepare to walk two miles (*my paraphrase*).

In negotiation, affirming your opponent's stance is one tool to disarm him. Playing the fool while focusing on the end product is an important tactic to win over an opponent.

"Step to their side," therefore, means playing along with a fellow disputant, with an aim to douse his anger and frustration. The end result of which is an amicable agreement. It is likened to a psychological redirection. The difference is that in redirection, the plan is to get the person exhibiting the behavior to focus on something else, different from the potential dangerous behavior.

In the same vein, "reframe" is a negotiation technique whereby one disputant changes the other from positional bargaining to problem-solving negotiation. "Reframing means taking whatever your opponent says and directing it against the problem" (Ury 1991, 84).

One rainy night, a rapist broke into a family home and ordered the female occupant to lie on the floor. The courageous woman first pretended to take off he top and suddenly turned to the rapist and suggested that they do it quietly in the bedroom. At that point, the rapist cringed, stopped yelling orders, and instead of going to the bedroom, quietly, beat a retreat toward the front door.

He was disarmed because contrary to his expectation of resistance, she softened up. He did not know what the woman was up against.

I was returning from a communion round (visit to the sick) and was driving a church marked Peugeot car in the twilight of one Saturday evening on an ever-busy 22nd Road in Festac, Lagos, Nigeria. At the intersection of 22nd and another busy street corner, a man called out, "Father (I was only a seminarian), can you give me a ride to the parish house, we have a prayer meeting." I did not recognize his face; I did not know everybody in a parish of more than five thousand families. I bet he did not know me, either; otherwise, he would not have called me "Father." He only recognized the church car. Anyhow, I picked him up. After we drove past the busy area, he asked me to stop him. I suspected he was up to something. I did not stop him, nor did I argue with him. I simply suggested he should not waste his bullet or waste his energy. I told him that I was willing to surrender the car keys quietly. He stared at me, speechless, as I kept driving slowly. When I got to the next busy junction, I stopped and he alighted. Before he got off, he looked straight in my eyes and remarked: "You are lucky." I did not know what I did to be *lucky*.

Looking back now, I can understand that he did not become violent because he felt I was willing to cooperate. In reality, I was not willing to give up the car just like that. My plan was to speed off with him to the nearest police station, making sure he did not struggle the steering with me.

BUILDING A BRIDGE

> Building a golden bridge means making it easier for your opponent to surmount the four common obstacles to agreement: It means actively involving him in devising a solution so that it becomes his idea, not just yours; it means satisfying his unmet interests; it means helping him save face; and it means making the process of negotiation as easy as possible.
>
> —Ury 1991, 91–92

In some sense, the concept of "building a bridge" is equivalent to the idea of *giving someone a rope to hang himself.* "Hanging" in this context is that the outcome of the decision is solely on the individual who accepts the suggestions and implements them. Resisting the urge to argue with the opponent is a strategy, which requires extra discipline, in order to achieve a common understanding. Not many decisions reached through this process are easily regrettable.

POWER TO EDUCATE

Education plays a vital role in virtually every aspect of human transaction and at every level of human development and existence. In negotiation, the "power to educate" is so important and has proven effective in negotiating a workable agreement. As a negotiation technique, "power to educate" enables one disputing party to let the other know the consequences of his/her inflexibility. It also allows the disputants to choose between options, which hitherto were not salient. The technique gives room for asking reality-testing questions: what do you think I will do? What will you do? These are the types of questions that elicit answers, which is where the *power to educate* comes in.

Politicians anywhere in the universe wear the same or similar garbs. For the purpose of the subject matter, Washington, DC, is a case study. It is no news that lawmakers try to outdo one another each time there is a fresh piece of legislation. In recent days, politicians have devised ways and means to hand-twist one another. One such example played out during the debate on extension of tax breaks and other matters.

Democrats, on one hand, asked questions bothering on what happens to the one hundred and sixty million (160,000,000) middle-class American workers who might see an average of twenty-dollar ($20.00) increase in their taxes if the break was not extended for two months. The Republican party, on the other hand, argued that two months' extension of such break was not just good for the tax-paying Americans.

At the end of the entire protracted debate, the Democrats used questions to *educate* the Republicans, using the argument of the hardships families would endure if their taxes went up in the New Year. Both parties also made compromises, thereby *building bridges* for each other to accede to a two-month extension of tax breaks for millions of Americans.

TURNING ADVERSARIES INTO PARTNERS

It is a natural reaction to meet force with force. When people are in conflict, the tendency is to outmaneuver the opponent, present a stronger argument and logic in order to win people's sympathy and in turn win the case. But in a negotiated settlement, almost the opposite is the case. In negotiation, moving against the current strengthens the resolve of the skilled negotiator. This means that instead of engaging in a natural flow of countering the opponent's position, you do the unexpected thing of tactically concurring with the opponent, thereby going against his adversarial expectation. This tactic is capable of disarming a hardened opponent.

In his book *Getting Past NO*, William Ury notes,

> Just as the best general never has to fight, so the police never had to use force. They used their power not to attack Van Dyke, but to contain him and educate him that his best alternative lay in surrendering peacefully. They brought him to his senses, not his knees.
>
> 1991, 143

This summary of a hostage encounter between the New York Police Department and a fugitive, Van Dyke, who escaped from the prison and took hostage of hospital employees, is a conglomeration of the entire five steps of breakthrough negotiation. The negotiator sounded like wonting to accede to the hostage taker's demands, yet not losing track of his mission. A good negotiator never gives up nor does he easily cave in under pressure. He uses all his skills to save an otherwise hopeless situation and to save both lives and save faces.

The concept of face-saving "refers to maintaining a good self image" (*Conflict Research Consortium*, University of Colorado). Some examples will further clarify the concept.

During the 2011 United States Republican Party presidential primaries, Herman Cain, a Republican presidential contender, addressed the press and announced the suspension of his presidential campaign. For an ordinary American, Mr. Cain suspended his campaign, period. But between him and his accusers, he tactically beat a retreat to avoid further embarrassment by the barrage of accusations of impropriety by different women. Mr. Cain probably adhered to Ury's recommendation that negotiators "go slow to go fast" (1991, 105). His moving slowly might have helped him trade minor concessions and focus more on what he gained (face-saving) than on what he lost by withdrawing from the campaign.

In September of 2004, a militant group in Russia invaded a school in Beslan, North Ossetia, taking hostage of students, teachers and guests. According to CBS News, "The terrorists wanted Russian President Vladimir Putin to announce the withdrawal of all troops from Chechnya."

The Russian authorities responded by moving in troops and tanks. At the end of the three-day siege, involving more than 1,200 hostages, "officials say 330 died—176 of them children. More than 500 others were wounded, and 24 children are now orphans" (CBS News).

The Russian government was not new to crises of that magnitude, nor was there any doubt regarding its capability to handle terrorism-related hostages. However, Russia's approach to the Beslan hostage standoff called to question its ability to effectively apply negotiation techniques.

Everything went wrong with the entire situation. The government moving troops and tanks challenged the hostage takers' power. The hostage takers did not have an escape route.

Since their demand was centered on the withdrawal of government troops from Chechnya, a skilled negotiator would *reframe* the militants' demand by tactically agreeing with them that the presence of the troops was inconveniencing. A skilled negotiator would *educate* them that the presence of troops in Chechnya was for the protection of the people's lives and property. The government should not have surrounded the school with tanks and armored personnel. Instead, a negotiator would have *built a bridge* by making a possible escape route for the hostage takers to exit the building when they got frustrated with the stalemate. At the end of the operation, the intention would not have been to *bring the militants to their knees, but to their senses.* This would have been achieved by letting them understand that the children have no place in government's decision to maintain troops presence in Chechnya, nor is the school part of government bargaining chip.

Since the hostage situation went on for three days, the militants certainly were hungry or sleepy at one point or the other. A negotiator would have *stepped to the side* of the militants by making sure they had something to eat or drink. They might shun the offer, but the idea of offering might be that magic moment, which would have saved hundreds of lives and helped both militants and government to save face.

PSYCHOLOGICAL LEGITIMACY OF MEDIATION

Mediation is a concrete human endeavor, impacting human behavior. Therefore any study of mediation must involve elements of psychology relevant to aspects under discussion. One such aspect is the importance of "logotherapy" in conflict resolution.

Viktor Emil Frankl developed logotherapay coined from Logos, a Greek word, which denotes meaning. He wrote about logotherapy thus: "The freedom of will; the will to meaning; the meaning of life, these are the concepts upon which logotherapy is based" (Frankl 1988, 7).

Quoting Graber, Chan writes of Viktor thus, "He was an intellectually precocious child…even before finishing high school, he had begun a scientific correspondence with Sigmund Freud" (2007, 32). He received his doctor of medicine degree in 1930 from the University of Vienna. He thereafter continued his training in neurology at the Psychiatric University Clinic.

One rather outstanding achievement of Dr. Frankl is his ability to galvanize hope for the seemingly hopeless young people of the poverty-stricken era in his country. After the Great Depression, he began to set up counseling centers in Austrian cities in 1930, primarily for students and the unemployed (2007, 34). Viktor got enmeshed in the Nazi onslaught in 1942; almost his entire family perished in the hands of the Nazis. He survived the concentration camp because his camp was liberated in 1945.

According to Chan, logotherapy focuses on the meaning of human existence as well as on man's search for such meaning (2007, 38). Although logotherapy is placed in the same psychotherapeutic category as existentialism, Frankl further describes it in these words:

> In contrast to most of the existentialist schools of thought, logotherapy is in no way pessimistic, but it is realistic in that it faces the tragic triad of human existence: pain, death and guilt. Logotherapy may justly be called optimistic, because it shows the patient how to transform despair into triumph.
>
> 1988, 9

This last point brings me to the realization that logotherapy is more concrete and directly influences human behavior. It directly applies to mediation practices.

Citing Irmeli Sjolie, Chan stipulates the three pillars of logotherapy as follows:

> 1. Life has meaning under all circumstances.
> 2. People have a will to meaning.
> 3. People have freedom under all circumstances to activate the will to meaning and to find meaning.
>
> 2007, 39

From the above stipulations, I believe that there is no universal application to the "rule." There are some individuals who hold to the fact that they are born into a certain situation, and there is nothing they can do to change it. In this case, the statement that "[p]eople have freedom under all circumstances to activate the will to meaning and to find meaning" does not necessarily apply. Again, what about people whom the society classifies as frustrated? These are people, who have practically reached the end of the street, and for them, life has no meaning, and there is no need struggling to change things around because it is not going to yield any meaningful fruit. Dr. Frankl, buttresses this position as quoted by Chan thus,

> Every individual is endowed with freedom, but because of the finiteness of the human being, there are some limitations to freedom in addition to other aspects of humanity…the freedom of man is a freedom within limits.
>
> 2007, 39

On the other hand, "Frankl asserts that each person is ultimately self-determining. This gives each individual the freedom to change the direction of his or her life; and, consequently self-determine who one will become" (2007, 40).

There is no doubt that individuals are self-determining, but various factors contribute to this situation. For instance, the general assumption is that people who live in conflict-prone regions perpetuate themselves and their offspring to the idea that they have to engage their neighbors in constant struggle in order to stay relevant. They therefore make little effort to wriggle themselves out of that situation because they believe that it is in their nature. At other times, people struggle on their own to address conflicts. Due to the lack of assistance occasioned by international bureaucracy, coupled with the fact that mediation involves other disputants who may not always agree to a resolution, such efforts get frustrated and disputants return to *status quo ante*.

Another poignant issue in Frankl's theory is the *Existential Vacuum*. It "manifests itself mainly in a state of boredom...a sense of *meaninglessness and emptiness*...an inner void...and apathy. If it persists in a person...it progresses into existential frustration...We try to fill the existential vacuum with drugs, violence, also with food, over-work, sports...yet remain unfulfilled" (2007, 51–52).

This aspect is usually helpful in today's family mediation. Many a home has either broken or remained dysfunctional due to the *existential vacuum* of its members. Some attribute it to economic factors; others believe it is all about dissatisfaction in relationships. Irrespective of the reason/s, the end product is that individual members resort to some kind of escape route out of their frustration, including the use of drugs, violence, and other societal vices. Some even vent their frustration on the entire society by resorting to armed robbery, rape, and other illicit activities.

Dr. Frankl seemingly implicates education when he writes,

> In an age of existential vacuum, we have said, education must not confine itself to, and content itself with, transmitting traditions and knowledge, but rather it must refine man's capacity to find those unique meanings, which are not affected by the crumbling of universal values. This human capacity to find meaning hidden in unique situations is conscience. Thus education must equip man with the means to find meanings. Instead, education often adds to the existential vacuum.
>
> —Frankl 1988, 85

A lot of educated people are highly depressed and find little meaning in life. Little wonder that this is the case. Science and technology have contributed immensely to the advancement of the modern man. In the same token, they have *conspiratorially* destroyed the mysteries surrounding human existence, thereby reducing man to merely a consumer of goods and services. Most of the things human beings produced—including services they provided, which gave them a sense of dignity, satisfaction, and productivity—have been assigned to robots and computers. What then is left for the idle man? Suicide, homicide, terrorism, armed robbery, genocide because he is frustrated and finds little meaning and reason for existence.

The Arab region with rich cultural diversity is capable of harnessing the rich potentials of its teaming youth who resort to violence due to the effect of existential vacuum and unguarded indoctrination. It was the failure of the old brigade to positively engage the people that partly gave rise to the Arab Spring.

One way of unifying the populace or at least enlightening the people is to reach out to schools to incorporate diversity awareness in their curricula. It is not just enough to start early to teach children the recital of the holy books. If their knowledge of the holy books were combined with their sense of unity, the Arab world would regain its glory as the region with rich cultural and educational base. This will in turn bring about lasting peace and security as well as prosperity in the region, free of superstition. This is a project expected of the new Arab Spring leaders.

Dr. Frankl also developed what he termed the three psychotherapeutic techniques in logotherapy, namely: Socratic Dialogue; Paradoxical Intention; Dereflection.

The Socratic Dialogue "helps to bring the therapeutic process to the core issue of 'where is the meaning in your life?'" The whole aim is to "make client independent of the therapist by helping him find his guidance within" (2007, 54).

In Paradoxical Intention, the patient is encouraged "to do, or wish to happen, the very things he fears engenders an inversion of intention. The pathogenic fear is replaced by a paradoxical wish" (2007, 54–55).

Dereflection strengthens our capacity for self-transcendence—our ability to reach out beyond self-centeredness toward other people or goals that are meaningful to us (2007, 56). Community service and other charitable acts are some of the virtues that can *dereflect* a patient from hyper-reflection. At this instance, the patient's focus is redirected to positive activities beneficial to other members of society, including the elderly, the poor, and helpless children. In the process, the patient gets some measure of healing by focusing on reaching out to other people instead of focusing on his/her own problems, which could be overwhelming.

The relevance of all these to mediation is that for disputants to find meaning in life, they must struggle to go beyond those aspects that stand between their personal pride (positional bargaining) and the general interest of the community. It is at this level that mediation begins. Mediation is a personal decision which starts from within the individual disputant's resolve to discuss the problem.

According to Frankl, "Logotherapy's concept of man is based on three pillars, the freedom of will, the will to meaning, and the meaning of life" (1988, 16). He continues, "Man's freedom is no freedom from conditions but rather freedom to take a stand on whatever conditions might confront him" (1988, 16).

Frankl infers, "But there is a difference between the attitudes one chooses to pain and guilt, respectively...fate cannot be changed...man, however, may well change himself..." (2007, 73). This quote is expressed in different contexts, but I put it as a whole because it talks about *attitudes* and *change*.

Suffice it to say that logotherapy is more of a catalyst than anything. It does not prescribe solution, but directs the individual toward finding solution and meaning based on life experiences and situations. It "is concerned with the patient's existential aspiration and frustration" (2007, 68).

Chan cites Viktor Frankl as writing that pacemakers "confront us with meanings and values...[peacemakers] alleviate the burden of meaning confrontation" (2007, 61). In either case, the mediator is involved in the psychological existence of human kind.

In mediation, the mediator assists the disputants to move into the *noetic* dimension. "This," according to Chan, "is where they are able to engage each other with intentionality and creativity in solving their problem, based on their ethical sensitivity, activation of conscience, understanding of values, and search for meaning" (2007, 65).

It could be inferred that mediation is synonymous with peacemaking, and that peacemakers must at all times and at all levels remain neutral and have a positive outlook toward the success of mediation. In some cases, this whole principle seems not to enjoy universal applicability.

For instance, when Saddam Hussein of Iraq annexed Kuwait, the United Nations intervened at the level of mediation. Mediation had hardly crumbled or come to a deadlock before the allied forces sent troops into Iraq, an action which eventually culminated in the hanging of Saddam and others.

In my imperfect but logical opinion, both Saddam and the people of the region were not allowed to exercise their "ethical sensitivity, activation of conscience, understanding of values, and search for meaning" (2007, 65). I wonder whether the mediators were able to exhaust their strategies before the bullets started ricocheting. I would give Saddam a chance to explain his action. I would engage in a shuttle diplomacy between Saddam and the Kuwaitis to see how best to resolve their conflict.

"A good mediator helps the parties in a dispute to discover the wisdom which they brought to the mediation, and to articulate it" (2007, 72).

From the example of Saddam Hussein, it could be understood that mediation applying the Franklian principle would handle the situation differently. A logotherapeutic mediator would assist the leader to discover for himself the meaning of his action, the outcome and implication in his leadership, in his personal life and in the lives of the citizens. At the end of it, they make an informed choice which could be either wrong or right. But most often would lead to right choices because it also involves conscience formation. As Thomas Aquinas would admonish that people should follow their conscience because an informed conscience never goes wrong. The human capacity to find meaning hidden in unique situations is conscience (1988, 85).

While mediation and logotherapy share certain commonalities, their aim and purpose differ. "The main goal in mediation is peace with an agreement between the disputants while that of logotherapy or Franklian psychology is the discovery of meaning through change of attitudes" (2007, 72).

I have informally mediated in a number of parent-child conflicts. The most recent was a case of a child who played truancy in school. Her parents believed that she went to school every day. Instead, the child would go loiter at a local shop and came back when she knew school was over. She was not lucky all the way. She soon fell prey to child predators. When eventually she was discovered, it was too late for her to claim innocence anymore. Her parents were angry with her on one side, she was angry with herself for her mistakes on the other hand. Parents asked her to leave their home.

When I intervened through the instrumentality of a Catholic group, I helped the child realize her folly as well as made parents understand the implications of sending her out of the house. We did not go all out to analyze what went wrong. Instead, I presented the realities of the situation from the viewpoint of the mistakes made by the child as well as the resultant effect of sending her out in the dark. At the end of the meeting, both parents and child literally forgot the truancy case and focused on remedying the triggers of the child's behavior.

The main fact of logotherapeutic technique is to help the patient to face the worst of his/her fears and anxiety. In colloquial terms, it is often said that things get worse before they get any better. My mother once told me a story of how curious I was even as a toddler. She said I liked the blue flame of the paraffin lantern. I would crawl up to the lamp stand, climb the chair, and tried to catch the flame. She was so alarmed that I would burn myself. No matter how she tried to keep me away from the lamp, I would cry and try the next minute to catch the flame. One day she watchfully left me alone to touch the flame. I touched the flame and was scalded. Then I cried and shrieked to the point that I became feverish. According to her, that was the end of my attempt to try to catch the flame ever again. As an adult I still take some stupid risks, but for some other reasons.

My mother was not a logotherapist, but she started using logotherapeutic techniques long before the publication of Dr. Frankl's book. It worked for her; I believe it would work for experts even more; only the correct application can do it.

Logotherapy struggles to help people find meaning, fulfillment, contentment, and purpose in life. Logotherapy, for me, is more pragmatic than some other psychological principles, especially as pertains to mediation. There is no doubt that all the psychological principles have their relevance in human existence. But borrowing the words of George Orwell, "All animals are equal, but some are more equal."

TERRORISM

It is often believed that the promise for "seventy black-eyed virgins" in paradise is an irresistible allurement which spurs men to take to suicide terrorism. But it takes only a greedy and less intelligent young man to fall for that. To manage one black-eyed virgin is already a tedious job. To think of managing seventy of such species is insane. Again, thinking about it, if paradise is a peaceful and holy place as we understand it, how would a holy and peace-loving God set up a chaotic and promiscuous situation just to reward the suicide bomber after destroying God's creation on earth?

Neither the Arab world nor the Middle East has a monopoly of violence. The menace of terrorism has become so widespread that insecurity has become the order of the day allover the human world. Did terrorists hijack any aspect of the Arab Spring? Could mediation have been employed in advance of any intended terrorist activity? These are rhethorical questions which might not get answered even by the perpertrators of the Arab Spring protests.

A couple of definitions of terrorism will go a long way in demystifying the secrecy enshrouding the act of terrorism. Not that terrorism is a right or wrong way of addressing grudges, but the different definitions are a representation of how the various organizations and individuals perceive it. The so-called terrorists might have a different definition of their act. What is called terrorism thus seems to depend on one's point of view (Hoffman, Jenkins).

In his book, *Inside Terrorism*, Bruce Hoffman observed that terrorism has undergone certain fundamental changes in meaning. He remarked thus, "The word 'terrorism' was first popularized during the French Revolution. In contrast to its contemporary usage, at that time, terrorism had a decidedly positive connotation" (Hoffman 2006, 3).

According to Hoffman, the Federal Bureau of Intelligence (FBI) defines terrorism as "the unlawful use of force or violence against persons or property to intimidate or coerce a Government, the civilian population, or any segment thereof, in furtherance of political or social objectives" (Hoffman 2006, 31).

The Department of Homeland Security (DHS) defines terrorism as "any activity that involves an act that: is dangerous to human life or potentially destructive of critical infrastructure or key resources: and…must also appear to be intended (i) to intimidate or coerce a civilian population; (ii) to influence the policy of a government by intimidation or coercion; or (iii) to affect the conduct of a government by mass destruction, assassination, or kidnapping" (Hoffman 2006, 31)

Terrorism, according to the Department of Defense, is "the calculated use of unlawful violence to inculcate fear; intended to coerce or to intimidate governments or societies in the pursuit of goals that are generally political, religious, or ideological objectives" (Hoffman 2006, 31).

Hoffman in his conclusion defined terrorism as "the deliberate creation and exploitation of fear through violence or the threat of violence in the pursuit of political change" (Hoffman 2006, 40).

What I could deduce from the various positions so far is that terrorism is a tool used by an individual or group of disgruntled elements to vent their bottled resentment and express frustration against an establishment's real or perceived injustice. Terrorism in this case could be targeted at the hapless citizens in order to embarrass their government. It could be directed at government officials for formulating policies not palatable to certain elements in society. At other times, terrorism could be directed toward the destruction of government or individual properties with the aim to attract attention, garner sympathy, and to make a point.

But the fundamental question remains whether or not these acts of terrorism could have been peacefully negotiated before they spiraled out of control.

Acts of terrorism do not just spring from the blues, they are triggered by certain factors: real or imagined. Human beings, not spirits, perpetrate acts of terrorism. But the clandestine nature of terrorism makes it hard for authorities to easily trace their source, and therefore, the reason/s behind terrorism. Some of the reasons, I believe, people resort to terrorism are as discussed herein.

INJUSTICE

From my understanding of terrorism, injustice seems the main reason people engage in terrorism. Acts of violence committed by groups that view themselves as victimized by some notable historical wrong often constitute terrorism.

According to *Merriam-Webster* dictionary (2011) "injustice means an act that inflicts undeserved hurt. Injustice applies to any act that involves unfairness to another or violation of one's rights."

In my understanding, terrorism could be a commensurate reaction to acts of oppression, repression, or denial of due rights of a people or of an individual by authorities of an establishment.

FRUSTRATION

Frustration is defined as "a deep chronic sense or state of insecurity and dissatisfaction arising from unresolved problems or unfulfilled needs" (*Medical Dictionary*, 2011). Any frustrated person is capable of engaging in any form of deadly activity to get his/her message across. If, for instance, a government is insensitive to the aspirations of an interest group, this could mark the beginning of conflict between the government and the group. Oftentimes, such conflict breeds terrorism.

JEALOUSY

Jealousy is defined as "resentment against a rival, a person enjoying success or advantage, etc., or against another's success or advantage itself" (Dictionary.com, 2011).

It is factual that some countries are more economically and technologically prosperous than others. In an effort to create a state of equality (as defined by them), a group of individuals might gang up against the prosperous nation. The group might even accuse the nation of contributing to their own woes, hence the justification to embark on property destruction and hostage taking, for ransom, leading to terrorism.

FANATICISM

Fanaticism is the attempt to repress elements of one's own being for the sake of others. If the fanatic encounters these elements in somebody else, he fights against them passionately, because they endanger the success of his own repression (Tillich 2011).

Religious zealots under the guise of defense of their religious belief carry out acts of terrorism to intimidate people into accepting their faith.

INTIMIDATION

Intimidation is "to make timid; fill with fear; to coerce or inhibit by or as if by threats" (*The Free Dictionary*, 2011).

Government is saddled with the responsibility of protecting its citizenry. And in this regard, any credible government arrests and prosecutes violators of the laws of the land. Yet in almost every nation on earth, there exist pressure groups whose whole aim is to protect its members against government oppression. These groups tend to run a parallel government within the government. To influence law enforcement, in order to get away with crime, some groups try to intimidate the government by engaging in acts of terrorism.

Intimidation and embarrassment of government are paramount instruments of terrorism. Although these groups have no formal connection with governments, they usually have the financial and moral backing of sympathetic governments.

Typically, they stage unexpected attacks on civilian targets, including embassies and airliners, with the aim of sowing fear and confusion. (*The American Heritage New Dictionary of Cultural Literacy*, 2005).

IS EVERY ACT OF TERRORISM PEJORATIVE?

I ask because there are various shades of official injustices and brutalities replete in today's society. If some people do not stand up and defend themselves, the more powerful and influential groups will try to obliterate them.

As a peace-loving, nonviolent advocate of human freedom from oppression, intimidation, exploitation, and injustice, I have come to observe that some governments do not believe in peaceful negotiation. Given this type of situation, terrorism, if targeted at the oppressor, could be justified. In this case, terrorism is not pejorative.

Currently, the Syrian forces and rebels are fighting for authority. The rebels, backed by their sympathizers and some mercenaries are employing every available military and non-conventional tactic to puncture and deflect the authority of the government. Although the rebels are fighting a legitimate government, their action could be justified by the fact that the government refuses to listen to the people's yearning for change.

Terrorism—anywhere, anytime, on anyone—is condemnable and pejorative. However, since human beings are created equal, any act that deprives individuals of this God-given equality and freedom must be met with commensurate resistance, including acts of terrorism. There is no justification for taking another person's life. But if a tyrannical regime engages in the act of terrorizing other human beings, the people involved have the right to defend their existence, even if it involves engaging in acts of terrorism against an oppressive regime.

Suicide attacks have become so widespread as an instrument of terrorism. Suicide attack in terrorism is equivalent to gorilla tactic in military warfare—the damage is done before the attacker is detected.

> Increasingly, Palestinians are coming to see suicide attacks as a strategic weapon, a poor man's *smart bomb* that can miraculously balance Israel's technological prowess and conventional military dominance. Suicide bombings give them something no other weapon could: the ability to cause Israel devastating and unprecedented pain.
>
> —Luft 2002

Suicide is the process of purposely ending one's own life. Suicide is viewed differently according to culture and religion. Some societies consider suicide honorable in certain cases, while other societies may treat it as a crime. Some people commit suicide out of frustration and despondency, while others commit suicide to prove their strong faith in their cause.

In certain African cultures, suicide is a taboo, an offense against the gods, neighbors, and relatives. The culture views anyone who commits suicide as being possessed by the evil forces. Therefore, his/her remains are not buried like every other dead. The remains are committed to the evil forest, without the necessary burial rites. The people believe that the deities are not happy with the dead, and therefore, not deserving of their protection (it is the people's belief that the deities protect both the living and the dead).

However, elsewhere in the world, suicide could be a heroic act, deserving of praise and the necessary accolade. For instance, Palestinian society lauds martyrs (suicide perpetrators) for their bravery and selflessness. Typically, candy is distributed in the streets and women respond with traditional shrieks of joy (Hoffman 2007, 158).

In recent years, suicide has become an indispensable instrument of protestation. It has been used in Chechnya and Yugoslavia, Jews and Arabs in Israel, Al-Qaeda and the United States interests, Boko Haram and Nigerian interests, just to mention a few.

Suicide is known to be cost effective as an instrument of war. Except in the United States, where Bin Laden's Muslim extremists flew planes into the twin towers and the Pentagon, most other ones have only involved individuals adorning the deadly vest. Even at that, it was little cost to the terrorists because the planes were hijacked. America lost human and material while the suicide perpetrators lost just men, which according to their sponsors is a just price to pay for their mission.

In my opinion, suicide is cowardice. Some of the perpetrators are young innocent teens that have been brainwashed. Their sponsors hardly undertake such missions themselves. They, like army generals, are the last to die in any warfare. If these "generals" are not prepared to wear the vests themselves, why do they go about recruiting other people to wear them? If these suicide sponsors have nerves, they should confront their opponents in a more civilized manner. They can either test their military might in an open combat or taken their matter to arbitration.

Dialogue and mediation remain the most effective means of addressing any concerns. Instead of taking to suicide and other clandestine means of redress, terrorists should openly address the bone of contention in civilized forums. The United Nations has been a big time mediator in international conflicts. Terrorists should first bring their grievances to the world body before venting their frustration on their opponent—if it comes to that.

Even at the deadlock of mediation, there is still no justification for suicide bombing. The evil of suicide bombing is quite enormous. It involves taking innocent lives—both of the victims and the (naïve) recruit suicide bomber.

In the civilized world, individuals express their grievances through the court or by bringing them to mediation and arbitration. In the terrorism world, jungle justice reigns. Most acts of terrorism are nocturnal and clandestine. Often, the perpetrators are faceless. Therefore, they hardly express their agitation before carrying out their nefarious activities.

From their account, terrorists feel that they are unfairly persecuted. As a way of remaining relevant and currying sympathy, they engage in terrorism. An example is a statement credited to the Palestinian terrorist team at the wake of the 1972 Munich Olympic massacre. It states, "we are persecuted people who have no land and no home land…why should the whole world be having fun and entertainment while we suffer with all ears deaf to us?" (Hoffman 2007, 235).

Some terrorist groups see themselves as sent by God to liberate humanity. They believe that their mission is to defeat the enemy—the oppressor—and obtain victory for the common people. This claim is not always (nor has it been) the case. Oftentimes, terrorists end up hurting the people they claim to protect.

When the Niger Delta militant groups in Nigeria began their agitation for some share in the oil revenue, many people were sympathetic to their cause. They blew up oil pipelines; sabotaged government interests along the creeks, including commandeering of barges and ocean liners along the coastal region; made the mangrove swamps inaccessible to government forces. They asked people to boycott government activities. They also asked people to revolt against the government. The gullible citizenry complied with the militants' directives. But this compliance lasted for as long as the militants' cause sounded genuine.

As the agitation progressed, criminal elements infiltrated the ranks of the militants. They took hostage of government officials, oil workers and civilians alike. They deviated from their original mission of service to the deprived Niger Deltans and resorted to selfish kidnapping of people for ransom. They engaged in all kinds of atrocities ranging from robbery to rape. They gradually lost their identity as representatives of the deprived and exploited public. The people stopped seeing them as heroes as much as they more and more became the people's nemesis.

Some terrorist groups are constant attention seekers. Insofar as they get publicity, they keep terrorizing the populace. Newsprint and airtime are thus the coin of the realm in the terrorists' mind-set, the only tangible or empirical means they have by which to gauge their success and assess their progress. In this respect, little distinction or discrimination is made between good and bad publicity. The satisfaction of simply being noticed is often regarded as sufficient reward (2007, 247).

In the commercial world, it is often said that "if you do not say you are here, no one will ever notice your presence." This is the power of advertising. Terrorists take advantage of media publicity in perpetrating violence. If the media should ignore terrorist activities, there is the likelihood that terrorism will reduce.

Terrorists are described as a "small group of individuals living underground, in close proximity to one another, constantly on the run and fearful of arrest and betrayal." Because they are not sure of even one another, they must possess good intelligence. Armed with good intelligence, they are able to decipher activities in and around their camps. They can plan and execute terror undetected.

Osama bin Laden was recently detected and eliminated having lived in Pakistan for an unspecified number of years. He and his terror group were able to plan and execute terror activities from his residence because he had good intelligence. On the flip side, every piece of *good intelligence* has an expiration date. A little hole along the line of transmission is capable of ruining, in one split second, a whole year's planning. This could come in the form of sabotage by an aggrieved member of the group or a concerned member of the civil society. I believe that was bin Laden's waterloo.

Terrorists could sometimes be mistaken for spirits. They tend to act in mysterious ways. However, when their network is busted, they are known to be cowards who live under the shadow of a large group whose stock in trade is to instill misery and destruction in society.

Some terror groups might have genuine grudge against their opponent, but they lack the courage to present their issue in a civilized manner. Since their supposed opponent has no idea what they are agitating for, it is difficult to even discuss with them. Again, some governments believe it is weakness to negotiate with terrorist groups. But if anything we hear in the news is correct, Hamid Karzai, president of Afghanistan, was cited to have confirmed that the United States government was discussing with Taliban (Fox News, June 18, 2011), a terrorist group believed to fraternize with al-Qaeda—the father of all terrorist groups. This, therefore, shows that terrorism has come to stay as part of the political spectrum.

Terrorism is not a congenital disease. No one is born a terrorist. Situations force people to take to terrorism. I beg to differ that terrorism is in the gene. Osama bin Laden's progeny, for instance, have no business being terrorists if they are not inclined to be. All I have heard about bin Laden's family is that it made a fortune from the construction industry. I have not read anywhere that bin Laden was from a family that made a living from terrorism. If he were not inclined to become a terrorist, bin Laden would have continued the family's trade—construction. That he took to terrorism does not mean that he inherited it from his father or was born with radicalism in his blood. Something pushed him into it.

To negotiate effectively with terrorists, the root cause of their action must be known and addressed. Hostage negotiation is the process of trying to align two often completely polarised parties. Authorities view hostage taking as unacceptable demands made by unacceptable means. However, terrorists view their actions as completely justified, even on moral and religious grounds. If they are to try and reconcile these two sides, it is essential for hostage negotiators to understand terrorist culture, the hostage takers' profiles, their personality, their view of the world, and also the authorities, their values, and their framing of the problem raised by the taking of hostages (Faure, Zartman).

In the history of terrorism negotiation, it has not gone without its own human and material costs. This has been for numerous reasons ranging from wrong negotiation approach to lack of understanding of the mind-set of terrorists.

In the health sector, prescriptions are made based on the outcome of diagnostics. It is often said that to find the cause of a problem is to have a solution to it. In order, therefore, to secure a meaningful negotiation with terrorists, they must be listened to, seen, and understood. Their opponent must be willing to discuss the issues objectively. The aggrieved must first be seen as human beings with concerns. The appellation, terrorist, should not be a barrier to negotiation. Just as we should not address a defendant as a prisoner or a criminal until he/she is convicted and sentenced, so we should not term the aggrieved "terrorist" until we have a concrete reason to.

If I found myself at war with terrorists, I would do a couple of things to negotiate a peaceful settlement. First, I would like to know the reason/s behind their action. I would weigh their reason/s with relevant societal norms. Do such reasons favor the majority of the populace, or driven by selfish ambitions?

Depending on my sociological disposition, I would spot their influential figurehead and request an audience with him/her. Representatives of both parties should moderate this meeting. If I were a representative of the government of the day, I would ensure that the terrorist is granted a safe landing, irrespective of the outcome of the negotiation. The need for this is to encourage others who might nurse grudges against the society to present them in a civilized manner, instead of taking the law into their own hands, thereby breed terrorism.

If I were the president of my country confronted with terrorists' demand for takeover of the government, I would not roll out the nation's armament. My first approach would be to address their demand by asking them to test their popularity by putting their names on the ballot.

If their demand were economic in nature, such as the case between the Niger Delta militants and the Nigerian government, I would do exactly what the former president Yar'adua did. The government granted amnesty to the militants and traded their arms for cash and scholarships.

Struggle between organized terrorism and the civil society is not easily wished away. It takes patience, diplomacy, tactics, sacrifice, and some measure of humility. When there is a stalemate, parties wait for who will blink first. Someone has to take the initiative. It is the wise and mature party that backs down, not out of weakness, but for a peaceful coexistence in society. Peaceful coexistence is absolutely possible in the Arab world if people will patiently listen to each other in mediation.

RELIGION, SPIRITUALITY, AND THE ARAB SPRING

For any meaningful mediation in the Arab region, religion and the spirituality of the people must be taken into consideration. Mediators must familiarize themselves with the subject matter of religion and spirituality as it pertains to the Arab Spring. This is so that when the disputants express themselves, the mediator will know where they are coming from. The mediator will also understand the disputants' sensitive issues.

For clarity purposes, I will cite a few definitions of religion. Again, since religion is such a diverse phenomenon, it needs to be viewed from different angles by different people.

Religion is "a set of beliefs concerning the cause, nature, and purpose of the universe, especially when considered as the creation of a superhuman agency or agencies, usually involving devotional and ritual observances, and often containing a moral code Governing the conduct of human affairs" (Dictionary.com, *Unabridged*).

Another author characterizes religion in these words: "Religion is a set of rules that a certain sect of a society abides by…a religion is a human quest for fundamental answers… religion does teach the followers obedience, humility, self-denial, forgiveness and non-resistance" (Gaikwad 2010, 1).

Anthony Nwachukwu, defines religion from the purview of spiritual psychology as:

> A conscious awareness, integration and use of one's situations, health, music, suffering, sickness, death, sports, food, wears, environments, dispositions, achievements, failures, struggles, destinies, education, status, neighbors, friends, enemies, names them, in endless, timeless and perpetual adoration, devotion, thanksgiving and appreciations to one's source of being and life.
>
> —Nwachukwu 2010, 196

Relating religion and spirituality, Nwachukwu writes:

> One can be so religious without mindful of what it means to relate and care for others. It is only when one incorporates good work and behavior with theology that one aspires to spirituality (Nwachukwu 2010, 48).
>
> "The qualifying criteria for heavenly rewards," according to him, "are based on being practical and sensitive to the minutest needs of the least of society, the helpless, and those hidden poor stricken individuals in our streets who have nobody to care for them" (2010, 195).
>
> He admonishes that, "heaven demands truth, justice, equity and spiritual prosperity." In his "theological

> arithmetic," he formulates an equation in which he stipulates that "religion plus good work is equal to eternal success, and good work minus religion is still equal to eternal success. But religion minus good work equals to eternal loss" (2010, 195).
>
> Both spirituality and religion aim to take an individual towards the ultimate goal of life. A religion does so by spoon-feeding the individual. Religion gives the person set guidelines and asks him/her to follow. Often, religious beliefs instill fear of God in you and make you do things without questioning them. Spirituality is worship of self as it believes God resides in you and nowhere outside. The reasons to do so often remain unexplained. On the other hand, spirituality is an individual experience of the encompassing effect. A spiritual person finds his own way, travels it alone, and reaches there in a state of euphoria. Therefore, following a religion is doing a duty, whereas being spiritual is being who you are.
>
> —Gaikwad 2011, 1

The relationship between religion and spirituality is as enumerated:

1. Religion and spirituality both refer to man's desire to find inner peace or God, regardless of the terminology they use.
2. Religion employs literature and rituals in its worship whereas spirituality uses personalized prayer and meditation.
3. To an outsider, religion may seem all about ritual while spirituality avoids anything that can become meaningless through repetition.

4. The rituals of religion are meant to foster a community of believers that provide both spiritual and physical succor to its members while people who consider themselves to be only spiritual are generally left to their own devices.

—Manish 2011, 1

According to Austine Cline,

> Religion is spiritual and spirituality is religious. One tends to be more personal and private while the other tends to incorporate public rituals and organized doctrines. The lines between one and the other are not clear and distinct—they are all points on the spectrum of belief systems known as religion. Neither religion nor spirituality is better or worse than the other; people who try to pretend that such a difference does exist are only fooling themselves.
>
> —Cline 2010, 1

Having looked at the various aspects of religion, it becomes important that any mediator in the Arab conflicts must familiarize himself/herself with these definitions and aspects in the event that situations arise in the course of mediation whereby they have to decipher the reason/s behind people's actions.

Karl Marx, a twentieth-century German philosopher, stated that "religion is the opium of the people" or the "opiate of the masses". As an opiate of the masses, religion is an instrument for maintaining social stratification and for keeping the masses under control.

Many an epoch has produced religious gurus as well as religious bigots and zealots, fundamentalists, and terrorists. There have been numerous instances where religion has been used as an excuse to exterminate people of other faith. A living example is one between Jews and Muslims and Christians in Palestine. There are also such intractable inter-religious wars in Northern Ireland. Bosnia-Herzegovina, Sudan, to mention just a few.

"The war in Bosnia-Herzegovina," according to *Ontario Consultants on Religious Tolerance*, "was among three faith groups (Muslim, Roman Catholic, and Serbian Orthodox). The Serbian Orthodox Christian attack on Muslims was elevated to the level of genocide" (Robinson 2011).

"For the religious terrorist, violence is first and foremost a sacramental act of divine duty executed in direct response to some theological demand or imperative" (Hoffman 2007, 88). Some religious adherents are willing to jump off the Tappan Zee Bridge because their religious leaders order them to as part of their religious sacrifice. Some religious leaders therefore capitalize on the gullibility of their followers to manipulate their thoughts and actions.

Dr. Martin Luther King Jr., Nelson Mandela, and a host of other crusaders of civil liberties had a series of rallies, yet their mission was devoid of violence. No doubt, there were pockets of skirmishes resulting from those rallies, but the messengers themselves never directly or indirectly tried to instigate the people to terrorize the society. But many a religious leader has at one time or the other incited hatred and violence by the invocation of sections of theological claims to justify their action. Numerous examples abound. Ayatollah Khomeini's declaration of Islamic republic of Iran, 1979, "We must strive to export our revolution throughout the world" (2007, 89). This is believed to be at the root of the Iranian-backed Islamic terrorist campaign.

There is an aphorism: "give the dog a bad name to hang it". This is a tactic often employed by terrorist religious groups. Some of these denigrating and dehumanizing terms include name-calling, such as infidels, evil generation, descendants of the devil, and other unprintable names.

It is on record that Osama bin Laden described the bombing of the twin towers in New York on September 11, 2001 as an act of God and as a punishment on "infidel armies" who must "leave the land of Muhammad"—(probably alluding to America's support for Israel and the struggles in Palestine).

Bin Laden was quoted as saying:

> He whom God guides is rightly guided but he whom God leaves to stray, for him wilt thou find no protector to lead him to the right way...God Almighty hit the United States at its most vulnerable spot. He destroyed its greatest buildings. Praise be to God.
>
> 2007: 81

Although not a religious leader, bin Laden cites a portion of his holy book to justify his killing of people on American soil, be they Americans or foreigners, Christians, animists, atheists, Muslims, or Jews. He stopped at nothing to make America look bad in the eyes of the Islamic world, presenting the United States as an enemy of Islam.

Religious terrorism is traceable to virtually all kinds of human conflicts. The conflict might originally look civil in nature. As it escalates, its religious trappings gradually emerge. The Sudanese war was originally civil; later it became a conflict between the Muslim north and Christian south. In Nigeria, originally the war was civil, but as it escalated, it became divided between Northern Nigeria Muslims and

Biafra Christian south. If the Western world knew what they know now about religious terrorism, the outcome of the Biafran/Nigerian war would have been different.

"Intolerance breeds injustice. Injustice invariably leads to rebellion and retaliation, and these will lead to escalation on the part of both making reconciliation almost impossible" (Robinson 1999). This, in my opinion, poses a big challenge to modern day mediation and mediators.

The Arab Spring: Mediation and Peaceful Political Transition is such a complex and diverse topic traversing several spectra of humanity. Therefore, the subheadings below address some of the relevant topics akin to the psychological and physiological aspects of mediation as treated in this work. The relevance is that a clear knowledge and understanding of a situation is the beginning of the solution. Once a mediator is at home with these terms, he will know where the disputants are coming from, and prepare to meet them at their own level. The behavioral pattern of the disputants may not always exhibit, but a mediator with a foreknowledge of human behaviors will certainly work successfully with anyone, irrespective of their attitude to mediation.

"*Crisis intervention* refers to the methods used to offer immediate, short-term help to individuals who experience an event that produces emotional, mental, physical, and behavioral distress or problems" (*Encyclopedia of Mental Disorders*). Example: At the wake of the earthquake in Haiti, the United Nations dispatched humanitarian assistance to the crisis-stricken island in order to quell further crisis occasioned by the earthquake.

"*Conflict management* is the long-term management of disputes and conflicts, which may or may not lead to resolution" (The President and Fellows of Harvard College,

2010). Example: In the days leading to the outbreak of civil war between Nigeria and Biafra, the Quakers employed international mediation, to avoid an escalation in an already volatile situation (Bercovitch 2003, 200–201).

Conflict Prevention is reducing conflict that comes from behavior and ways of communicating that create unnecessary, unresolvable conflicts. It's about learning to say things in ways that do not get people's defenses up…It's a tool for the resolution of issue-based conflict, not a way of avoiding it (*Conflict*, 2010). Example: A truck bomb exploded at the World Trade Center in New York City on February 26 killing six people and injuring hundreds more. His (Clinton's) reaction was one of conflict avoidance—he said little about aggression of the enemy, nothing about blaming, and focused solely on hardship, mentioning the issue very briefly in his weekly radio broadcast… (Feste 2010, 17).

Conflict transformation usually denotes truth and reconciliation measures and commissions. Meetings form between factions of both sides that are able to peaceably talk to one another and efforts are made to promote understanding and empathy and stimulate healing of past harm done (Hope 2010). Example: The referendum, which gave rise to the "Good Friday Agreement" in Northern Ireland, was a result of a series of international mediations involving almost every major country in Europe and beyond.

SPECIFICS OF THE ARAB SPRING

Frustration with closed, corrupt, and unresponsive political systems has led to defections among elites and the fall of once powerful regimes in Tunisia, Egypt, and Libya (Goldstone 2011). Of all the three countries mentioned, Tunisia's Ben Ali seemed to heed the call and decided to literally live to fight another day. His temporary resistance was the reasonable thing to do at that moment. He however caved in to pressure when he realized that he was getting isolated as the days went by. He was a smart man because he was kicked out of office, went into exile, and continued his life instead of going to the great beyond like his contemporary, Quaddafi of Libya, who clung to power till death did him part.

Ben Ali's nemesis was Mohamed Bouazizi, a Tunisian street vendor, initially wrongly said to be a college graduate. He set himself on fire on 17 December 2010, in protest of the confiscation of his wares and the harassment and humiliation that he reported was inflicted on him by a municipal official and her aides. When the smoke settled, neither Bouazizi, President Zine el-Abidine Ben Ali, nor the entire Arab world had an inkling that that singular act of frustration, and to an extent, heroism, would result to a worldwide outrage, spreading like a summer wildfire to even the hitherto peaceful areas of the world.

Ben Ali had known crises in the past. He once "engaged in anti-French, pro-independence activity, acted as a runner between local Neo-Destour—a liberal, constitutional political party—activists and members of guerrilla bands. When his Neo Destour activities came to the attention of the French colonial administration, Zine Ben Ali was expelled from school and denied admittance to any French-administered school in the colony.

He later assumed the presidency of Tunisia from his prime minister position. He was alleged to have removed the aged Habib Bourguiba from the presidency, citing mental infirmity as the main reason for his action (Gale 2006).

Unlike Ali who abdicated, Muammar al-Qaddafi of Libya probably believed he was invincible. He came to power in September of 1969 after a coup against King Idris who was away for a medical treatment in Turkey. He exited power through a bloody and popular uprising culminating in his death. "After more than four decades in power, Qaddafi's downfall happened in less than a year" (A&E Television Networks 2012).

Qaddafi was probably a strong man, but his handling of the rebellion against his government was shabby, shameful, and unbefitting of an intelligent leader. During the campaign against his government, he was seen at several rallies and in company of a retinue of guards, various security men, and women armed to the teeth. He would yell and curse and threaten fire, hell, and brimstone. If all that was aimed at intimidating his opponents, it did not work. When they came for him, he was slaughtered like a festival ram.

Hosni Mubarak ruled Egypt between 1981—after the assassination of Anwar al-Sadat (former president)—to 2011 when the Arab Spring swept him off the grips of power.

In Egypt, said Merlyna Lim (a scholar of social transformation at Arizona State University), people shared a yearning to oust Hosni Mubarak, but each person was afraid to step forward. Once they saw how many other Egyptians agreed with them, they grew bolder (Saletan 2011).

> On January 25, 2011, Egyptian protesters began staging large-scale demonstrations throughout the country calling for Mubarak's resignation. The "Arab Spring" sought to remove dictators across the Middle East and the demonstrators in Cairo's Tahrir Square quickly gained international attention. Though aggressive actions by the protesters were rare at the start, violence in the streets quickly escalated between Mubarak supporters and the opposition following his announcement on February 1 that though he would not resign from the presidency but also would not seek another term in the elections scheduled for September 2011.
>
> —Bard, Berman, Dawson, Scheinerman, Snider

If his intention for such announcement was to appease the people, he rather infuriated them the more. Shortly after the announcement, Egyptians became more resolute in getting rid of his despotic government. Finally, he yielded to pressure and abdicated, and was later committed to a prison term.

Ali Abdullah Saleh of Yemen also had a bitter taste of the Arab Spring. He was lucky to get away with just an injury when his presidential palace was attacked by Yemeni protestors. He was forced to flee to Saudi Arabia. Through high-powered mediation, coupled with a good measure of gerrymandering, he considered it wise to handover power to his deputy.

> He [Saleh] made his way up the military's ranks and waited for his opportunities. In 1974, Ibrahim al-Hamdi, with Saleh's help, led a military coup that exiled President Abd-el Rahman al Iryani. Al-Hamdi was murdered in 1977. His successor was assassinated the following year. Saleh had worked with both. On July 17, 1978, Yemen's 99-member People Council elected Saleh president with 76 votes.
>
> —Tristam 2012

Saleh, in my judgement, was as wise as his Tunisian counterpart. He yielded to pressure, resigned or was kicked out. He is still living, but not in the presidential mansion.

Bashar al-Assad took over power in Syria at the death of his father. Bashar was originally trained as an ophthalmologist. His medical career came to an abrupt end when his older brother, who was groomed for the presidency, died in an accident.

Since coming into power, "Syrians and the rest of the world have been watching him very closely to see if Assad will follow in the footsteps of his father, a shrewd and uncompromising man who ruled Syria for nearly 30 years with an iron fist" (*Encyclopedia of World Biography*, 2004)

The direction of the Syrian revolution is not yet clear. What seems clear is the people's voice calling for the president's resignation. When similar voices were raised in other parts of the Arab region, the final outcome was in favor of the people who lived after the dust cleared to tell the story.

In Bahrain, the Sunni Al-Khalifa dynasty has ruled since 1820, emboldened by an 'informal treaty' signed with Great Britain granting the Al-Khalifa the official title of Rulers of Bahrain (Mihlar, Eastwood).

The political imbroglio in Bahrain is not abating any time soon. The conditions which gave rise to the advent of the crisis are practically institutionalized. For instance, there are claims that the protests are a direct reflection of the political marginalization and discrimination faced by the Shia community. It is also a result of the lack of reform and the fact that the dominant group has clung to power for life, to the detriment of the other groups, which consider themselves edged out of the national polity.

According to the Bahrain Center for Human Rights, Shia villages have higher levels of poverty and unemployment than Sunni villages. The protests in Bahrain are not targeted at the leadership as much as on the system that has institutionalized a particular dynasty.

To demonstrate that the Arab Spring is no respecter of territories, it spread beyond the borders of the region of origin and gave rise to other demonstrations against opulence, social and economic inequalities as in the case of *Occupy Wall Street* and other *Occupy* projects elsewhere in the world. Even sacred institutions as the British and Saudi monarchies were not spared.

Perhaps the Saudi Arabian king Abdullah was the smartest of the Arab rulers. Reports had it that his swift reaction to brewing protests saved the kingdom from Arab Spring embarrassments. But his perspicacity did not come without a price. At the notice of local agitations "Inspired by protests in other Arab countries,...[the monarch] unveiled

$37 billion in benefits for citizens in an apparent bid to curb dissent" (Laessing 2011).

"Death to the dictator" rent the air as protesters in Iran got frustrated with President Mahmoud Ahmadinejad. Ahmadinejad, who has been a taunt on the flesh of some Western powers, seemed unperturbed by the protests. To him, he had seen worst situations and had even been alleged to have taken part in the hostage taking at the American Embassy in Tehran. The allegation was vehemently denied.

Some of the former hostages have identified him as one of the student leaders involved in holding fifty-two (American) embassy employees for 444 days between 1979 and 1981. Ahmadinejad denies this, as do several of his political opponents who were involved in the embassy takeover.

Although the Arab Spring did not immediately sweep the government of Ahmadinejad, Western governments' sanctions was intended to make or mar the republic.

IRAQ, QUINTESSENTIAL OF ARAB SPRING

Some popular understanding is that if it could happen to Saddam Hussein, it could happen to just about any despot. Iraq's Saddam Hussein and his protégé were gone long before the waves of Arab Spring. Of course, the history of Arab Spring would not be complete without a mention of Iraq, because Iraq endured similar or worst fate, which drove the entire region to mass protests.

> In the aftermath of Operation Desert Storm, the United States encouraged Kurds and Shiites to rebel against Hussein's regime—then withdrew and refused to support them, leaving an unknown number to be slaughtered. At one point, Hussein's regime killed as

> many as 2,000 suspected Kurdish rebels every day. Some two million Kurds hazarded the dangerous trek through the mountains to Iran and Turkey, hundreds of thousands dying in the process.
>
> —Rosenberg 2012

That was only a minute fraction of crimes against humanity as ascribed to Hussein. He got away with all these atrocities at the watchful gaze of the civilized world. When world leaders eventually woke up from their deep slumber, they, like a drunken gunman, started shooting sporadically in the air, looking for probable reason to indict Saddam and in the process started a situation that worsened the lots of Iraqi people.

Even those opposed to his brutality believe that Iraq was more peaceful when Saddam was ruling. Various Iraqi citizens, young and old, poor and rich, ruling elite and the proletariats alike, have expressed this nostalgic sentiment at various points. According to Abbas Mehdi, a former advisor to Iraqi Prime Minister, Nouri al-Maliki, "It was much better in prewar times than today. In terms of security, Saddam [Hussein] was a criminal. But at least people used to go out, the schools were open..." (Bruno 2007, 1).

When the United States government decided to attack Iraq, little did they envisage the resultant devastating effect of the conflict. Prelude to this attack was the annexation in 1990 of Kuwait by Iraqi forces. It should be recalled that the "United Nations Security Council Resolutions 660 and 662 condemned Iraq's invasion and annexation and called for the immediate and unconditional withdrawal of Iraqi forces." These resolutions were subsequently followed by a response by the United States National Security Directive

45,...outlining US objectives: the "immediate, complete, and unconditional withdrawal of all Iraqi forces from Kuwait..." (Richelson 2001). This was the advent of Operation Desert Storm, which President Saddam tagged *mother of all battles*.

A few years later, the United States invaded Iraq, accusing it of stockpiling weapons of mass destruction as well as sponsoring terrorist groups. This culminated in the hanging of Saddam Hussein and a lingering conflict in the Persian Gulf.

From all enlightened indications, it seemed that the main reason the United States went to war in Iraq was to eliminate the oppressive regime of Saddam Hussein. In the same vein, it looked like the charges against the regime were trumped up—a case of giving the dog a bad name to hang it. The various governments of the so-called allies sooner than later realized that contrary to their reasons for going to war, the intelligence report was faulty in the first place.

Within the same period in question, Afghanistan became another military target of the United States. This attack was not as surprising as the one on Iraq. While Afghan government was accused of harboring terrorists who launched attacks on the United States, Iraqi government was believed to possess weapons of mass destruction and sponsoring terrorism: unfounded and false allegations. At least President Bush himself would later acknowledge, the biggest regret of all the presidency has to have been the intelligence failure in Iraq (Goldenberg 2008).

Tony Blair, whose regime as British prime minister, waged war against Iraq had some reservation regarding his choice of war over mediation in Iraq. He admitted failing to foresee the *nightmare* that unfolded after he committed British troops to the conflict in 2003 (Blake 2010).

Before going to war in Iraq, reputable world leaders warned against the idea. Both political and religious leaders voiced their condemnation of the unjust war. One such warning was by Pope John Paul II who spoke out against a possible war in Iraq.

War is not always inevitable. It is always a defeat for humanity. War is never just another means that one can choose to employ for settling differences between nations. War cannot be decided upon, except as the very last option and in accordance with very strict conditions, without ignoring the consequences for the civilian population both during and after the military operations (Cline 2012).

On March 21, 2003, a nonprofit, progressive, nonpartisan, political activist online site published a litany of condemnations of the war in Iraq.

French president Jacques Chirac was credited with saying that France regrets this action undertaken without the approval of the United Nations. President Vladimir Putin of Russia described the US-led offensive as a serious political mistake and called for an immediate halt to hostilities. German chancellor Gerhard Schroeder called war a defeat for politics and said a bad decision was taken. China, a UN Security Council permanent member also opposed to war, appealed to the relevant countries to stop the use of military force. India, another nuclear power, called the US-led attack a violation of the UN Charter. Mexican president Vicente Fox stated: We are against the war. Prime Minister Jean Chretien of Canada called the war unjustified.

In the Middle East, the Palestinian Authority strongly condemned the military campaign. Arab states, Jordan and Saudi Arabia said they were worried about the conflict in the region. In Beirut, Lebanese president Emile Lahoud warned:

We see this aggression today plunging the world into a tunnel where one cannot see the end. In Turkey, President Ahmet Necdet Sezer voiced opposition to the US-led war shared by the vast majority of Turks.

United Nations Secretary General, Kofi Annan, urged the United States and Britain to do everything possible to protect civilians from undue harm and suffering during their campaign to unseat Saddam (Brown, Queally, Germanos, Zimet, Shaughnessy). These warnings point to the fact that in a well-mediated conflict, war may not even be in the horizon.

In mediation, the mediator assists the disputants to move into the *noetic dimension*. "This," according to Chan (2007), "is where they are able to engage each other with intentionality and creativity in solving their problem, based on their ethical sensitivity, activation of conscience, understanding of values, and search for meaning" (Chan 2007, 65).

Mediation is synonymous with peacemaking; therefore, peacemakers must at all times and at all levels remain neutral and have a positive outlook toward the success of mediation. However, recent world events tend to instill doubt in my mind about transparency and neutrality of mediation at certain levels. For instance, when Saddam Hussein of Iraq annexed Kuwait, the United Nations intervened at the level of mediation. Mediation had hardly crumbled or come to a deadlock before the allied forces sent troops into Iraq—an action which eventually culminated in the hanging of Saddam and others.

In my imperfect opinion, both Saddam and the people of the region were not allowed to exercise their ethical sensitivity, activation of conscience, understanding of values, and search for meaning (Chan 2007, 65). I wonder whether the mediators were able to exhaust their strategies before the bullets started ricocheting. I would give Saddam a chance to explain his action. I would engage in a shuttle diplomacy between Saddam and the Kuwaitis to see how we could come to terms with each other.

A good mediator helps the parties in a dispute to discover the wisdom, which they brought to the mediation, and to articulate it (Chan 2007, 72). Charles Taylor of Liberia was accused of instigating conflict on the West Coast of Africa. Nigerian government stepped up to mediate. As part of the mediation, Taylor was granted asylum in Nigeria. He had hardly settled down in his new residence before the international community accused him of causing trouble from his home in Southern Nigeria. As a result, the Nigerian government was coerced into sending him packing. In the process of leaving Nigeria, he was arrested and consequently flown to The Hague where his trial was recently concluded. Charles Taylor—though not a saint—was given a raw deal. I would doubt the transparency of both the Nigerian government and the international community. They seemed to have prearranged his arrest. I would make Taylor face justice, but would not trick him into initial effort towards mediation.

LEADERSHIP AND THE ARAB SPRING

Long before Saddam Hussein and the entire Arab Spring conflicts, the world had seen all kinds of leaders, ranging from the benevolent to the most malevolent. There have been protests and agitations for change, but the Arab Spring protests seemed the most organized and successful. This was attributable to the advent of social networks and the universal consciousness that leadership is supposed to be transient.

This study showcases a couple of past leaders and styles. These are randomly picked to build a case for different concepts of leadership and their applicability to the Arab Spring project.

ARISTOTLE

Every epoch produces human beings who influence aspects of the people's lives in a given society. Greece at one point was the cradle of human knowledge. Among the intellectuals of the time was Aristotle. He was so intelligent that he was single-handedly picked out to mentor/tutor a thirteen-year-old boy who later became Alexander the Great. His knowledge of almost everything the human mind could grasp makes him so outstandingly unique in every sense of the word. He is credited with educating the world. Though originally from Macedonia, Aristotle went to Athens to study under Plato.

When faced with possible execution, his repertoire of intelligence quickly kicked in, propelling him to flee from danger, as opposed to obstinately holding forth and be killed in the process. "Aristotle recalling the fate of Socrates…fled the city, saying that he would not give Athens a chance to sin against philosophy" (Hart 1992, 71).

Whether his flight was an act of cowardice or really for the reason he gave, he was really prudent. Saddam Hussein of Iraq had a similar premonition, as well as an opportunity to flee, but remained obstinate and paid dearly for it. Julius Caesar of the then Roman Empire remained obstinate till death. Col. Muammar el-Qaddafi of Libya stubbornly clung to power, irrespective of all danger signals. The summary is that every great thinker in history at some point escaped danger and still saved both face and life. He knew that it was not time for him to die, Jesus escaped from the Pharisees who plotted to kill him (Mat 12:14–16, NIV).

One prominent postulation of Aristotle was "…the notion that the universe is not controlled by blind chance, by magic, or by the whims of capricious deities, but that its behavior is subject to rational laws…" (Hart 1992, 70). This whole idea of "nothing in life is left to chance" is what spurs and motivates great innovators and inventors to be creative, irrespective of temporary and ephemeral obstacles. Thomas Aquinas's Five Ways: a proof of the existence of God was in consonance with Aristotelian theory of motion.

This aspect of Aristotelian philosophy, in my opinion, challenges the evolutionary theory. Aristotle would question the theory that human beings evolved from the apes as opposed to creation.

Another aspect of Aristotelian postulations worthy of note is the understanding that "Poverty is the parent of revolution and crime…the fate of empires depends on the education of youth" (Hart 1992, 74).

Aristotle understands the art of governance: feed the populace, empower the youth, and enjoy a peaceful reign. Many a government had fallen because the rulers ignored the Aristotelian principle of leadership. If Karl Marx believed that religion is the opium of the masses, Aristotle affirmed that education of the youth is a means to peaceful governance.

Aristotle lived for only sixty-two years, but his legacy lives on. Although he died in exile, the city of Athens would love to see him return to continue his contributions to human intellectual developments. He wrote books ranging from logic to metaphysics, science to the humanities. He was not strictly speaking a theologian, but his theories are the basis for many theological formulations.

If he lived in the modern day Arab region, Aristotle would try to empower the youths of the region, get them busy, educate them, keep them productive so that the Arab Spring would not even flash their occupied and busily productive lives.

CHRISTOPHER COLUMBUS

Christopher Columbus was born in Italy in 1451. He later became a ship captain and a navigator. An account has it that his attempt to find a westward route from Europe to the Orient inadvertently discovered the Americas. According to

Hart, Columbus's "discovery, which inaugurated the age of exploration and colonization in the New World, was one of the critical turning points in history" (Hart 1992, 47).

Of all the qualities that constituted this great man's popularity, Christopher Columbus's spirit of steadfastness is one capable of spurring anybody into action. His whole mission was a source of encouragement for anyone aspiring to greater heights.

One account had it that in his effort to discover the New World, Christopher Columbus faced a barrage of opposition from members of his own crew. Between September 6, 1492, when they left the Canaries, and October 12 when they sighted land, the sailors had pressured him to return to Spain, which they left since August 3 because they were frightened and the voyage was getting longer than expected. Because he was determined in his resolve to achieve his goal, he ignored such pressure and discouragement and continued with his journey.

Another aspect of his achievement worthy of note is that his discovery "opened to the people of Europe two new continents for the settlement of their expanding populations, and provide a source of mineral wealth and raw materials that altered the economy of Europe" (1992, 47).

When he set out in search of the land, little did Christopher Columbus know that he was going to discover the New World, part of which is the present-day continent of North America. Christopher Columbus comes on as a motivator, an achiever, one whose foresight produced one of the greatest continents on earth. His character is a type which poses a positive influence on the youth and on anyone who intends to make a name for himself and his community.

The downside of Christopher Columbus is that he "treated the Indians with shocking cruelty" (1992, 51). His discovery was said to have led to the destruction of the civilizations of the American Indians (1992, 47).

Evil is evil anywhere, anytime, and in any circumstance. But if Machiavellian dictum "the end justifies the means" is anything to cite, Columbus should not be outrightly condemned. He did what any prince has done and will be willing to do in order to accomplish a mission. Ethically, it is condemnable to destroy another person's heritage in order to build one's empire.

Christopher Columbus, in my opinion, represents everyone who aspires to greatness through selfless contributions to human civilization. Although his discovery of the Americas is believed to be accidental, that singular act of courageous voyage later gave rise to the birth of a great nation and the advancement of humanity.

Columbus featured because if he lived in the present-day Arab world, he would use his innovation to expand the region, which would douse most of the tensions relating to land borders in the region.

CHARLES SCHWAB

In 1921, Andrew Carnegie picked Charles Schwab to become the first president of the newly formed United States Steel Company. At the age of only thirty-eight, his salary was over one million dollars a year. When asked what qualified him to earn such large salary, he responded: "I consider my ability to arouse enthusiasm among my people the greatest asset I possess, and the way to develop the best that is in a person is by appreciation and encouragement" (Carnegie 1981, 53).

Charles Schwab was knowledgeable enough to be appointed the president of the steel company. However, he became popular not for his expertise in the field of steel production. He was rather paid highly due to his ability to galvanize his workers' morale and motivate them to fall in love with their work and to feel liked, appreciated, and wanted at work. This is a rare charisma which is needed to douse workplace stress and manage personnel to enhance productivity.

Let it not be a distraction that Schwab's name features in this section. It is strategically placed to demonstrate that even in the midst of chaos, there could be serenity. He was neither a politician nor a warrior. He rather made his mark in the area of organizational prowess. Charles Schwab became a leader simply by worming himself to the hearts of his subjects. Most Arab Spring leaders, to the contrary, forced themselves on the people who endured for as long as the elasticity of their patience lasted.

ROBERT MUGABE

Mugabe of Zimbabwe does not belong to the list of one hundred notable leaders on our purview. As a scholarly work, it is my prerogative to discuss him here. He earns a place in this book because part of the reason for the Arab Spring was a result of faulty intelligence and dangerous presumptions about the people and their leaders. Zimbabwe might suffer a similar fate if awareness is not created.

Although he has not been accused of terrorism or terrorism sponsorship, Mugabe has earned himself an unenviable title as an enemy of the West. But if all indices are placed right, this needs not be the case.

As far as the story goes, his one crime against the West is that he engaged in land redistribution which did not favor white farmers. The decision might be in bad taste, but what is leadership without taking into consideration the interests of the majority of the population? Again, no leader worth his salt is ever admired by every segment of his constituents.

Every notable leader first looks out for his/her own people before reaching out to the outside world. I would be slow to judge Mugabe if the issues between him and the West were based solely on land redistribution. Zimbabweans, white or black, deserve equal ownership of wealth. If Mugabe decided, in his wisdom, to allow every citizen a share in the nation's largesse, so be it.

NAPOLEON BONAPARTE

Napoleon was a French general and an emperor. He was born in 1769 and graduated from the French military academy in 1785. Napoleon's military exploits started at the age of sixteen. He achieved many successful military expeditions in several foreign countries. However, when he waged war in a failed effort aimed at the invasion of Egypt, his military might was rubbished by the intervention of the British navy. Napoleon abandoned his army in Egypt and returned to Paris. Napoleon later took over the leadership of France via a coup d'etat. He later edged out his fellow conspirators and became a de facto military dictator.

Napoleon fought and won many foreign wars, but the British military was one formidable force against his invasion and annexation of other countries. When he was restored to power after escaping from Elba, he met his final defeat at Waterloo. After Waterloo, Napoleon was imprisoned by the

British on St. Helena, a small island in the south Atlantic (Hart 1992, 185). He died there in 1821.

During the Napoleonic wars, it has been estimated that approximately five hundred thousand French soldiers died.

However, everything about the dictatorship of Napoleon was not negative. According to Hart, Napoleon was merely an ambitious opportunist, and he had no particular interest in perpetuating horrible massacres (1992, 186). He is credited with selling, in 1803, a vast tract of land to the United States. The Louisiana Purchase, perhaps the largest peaceful transfer of land in all of history, transformed the United States into a nation of near-continental size (1992, 187).

Napoleon is said to have reformed the financial structure and the judiciary. He created the Bank of France and the University of France. He reformed the French civil code. Under the code, there were no privileges of birth.

AUGUSTUS CAESAR

Augustus Caesar, formerly known as Gaius Octavius, was the grandnephew of Julius Caesar. He was born in 63 BC. He was an eighteen-year old student when his granduncle Julius Caesar, then the Roman emperor, was assassinated for intending to end the republican government and install himself a Roman monarch.

Certain conditions were favorable to Augustus Caesar's ascendancy to the Roman power. Julius Caesar, who did not have his own legitimate son, adopted Augustus as his son, and in turn had prepared him for a political career. Even when the empire became territorially divided between Augustus and Mark Antony, he skillfully won the support of some of Caesar's legions. Antony, who was overly distracted by his romance with Cleopatra, lost the war between him and Augustus. As a result, he committed suicide with his sweetheart, thereby becoming the last straw in Augustus's way to power.

The Roman people were obviously frustrated with the trend of events at this point. "After many years of civil war and the obvious failure of republican government in Rome, most Romans were willing to accept a benevolent despot, as long as the pretence of democratic rule was continued" (1992, 93). Augustus Caesar took advantage of this situation and played on the mentality of the people. "Though he had been ruthless during his fight to the top, [he] was surprisingly conciliatory once he was established in power" (1992, 93). It is said that "Augustus stands out as perhaps the best example in history of a capable, benevolent despot. He was a true statesman, whose conciliatory policies did much to heal the deep divisions resulting from the Roman civil wars" (1992, 96).

NAPOLEON BONAPARTE AND AUGUSTUS CAESAR

Napoleon Bonaparte was to France what Augustus Caesar was to Rome. Napoleon was not originally born in France, rather he was born in Corsica. Augustus Caesar, from every indication, was born into the Roman monarchy, being the grandnephew of Julius Caesar: the great Roman emperor. Both Augustus and Napoleon rose in ranks in the military and politics of Rome and France respectively.

From the foregoing, we see two important personalities who contributed immensely to world history and human advancement. Napoleon is credited with the liquidation of a good number of French soldiers and the oppression of neighbors who refused his advances. Augustus is known to have been so skillful and shrewd in his leadership style. While Napoleon's escapades were international in nature, Augustus was confronted mainly with domestic leadership struggles. Augustus calmed frayed nerves of the Roman people by instituting, in principle, a republican government, for which his uncle, Julius, was assassinated. Napoleon busied himself with attacking neighboring states in an effort to amass territorial and regional vastness. Augustus, on the other hand, used every instrument at his disposal to firmly secure his position as the founder of the Roman Empire.

Both men goofed in leadership. Both were brutal, dictatorial, authoritarian, and despotic in some ways. But the difference between the two lies in their levels of application. Napoleon applied brute force almost all the way. Augustus applied the wisdom, astuteness, and prudence acquired from his uncle who prepared him for the challenges of leadership.

Both leaders engaged in some measure of internal brutality on the people they were meant to protect. However, both contributed in no small measure to rewriting world history and (in the case of Napoleon) geography. Napoleon was the one who sold Louisiana to the United States. Therefore, making it possible for the United States to gain territorially from Napoleon's recklessness.

If they were contemporaries, the duo would probably have gained a lot from each other. Napoleon would have learnt from Augustus how to mix his brutality with some measure of humaneness. As a result, Napoleon would have emulated Augustus's leadership ingenuity and mingled his brutal regime with some measure of reconciliation. While France lost territories during Napoleon's era, Rome prospered under the leadership of Augustus.

ADOLF HITLER

History has it that Hitler's rise to power was partly influenced by the Great Depression of 1929. The depression and its aftermaths contributed to Hitler becoming German chancellor in 1933 at the age of forty-four.

"Hitler gained the genuine support of most Germans, because he was able to reduce unemployment and generate economic recovery" (Hart 1992, 206).

Hitler's German economic prosperity as well as his military dexterity, coupled with the economic woes of superpowers like France and England, drove him to attack and conquer many European nations, including the Soviet Union, which was ruled by another dictator of almost equal trepidation. Hitler's thirst for territorial grabs was not just limited to European nations; the United States had a fair share of his bid to conquer the world. In December of 1941 he declared war on the United States. However, Hitler's military valor came crashing after losing his battle for Egypt and Russia. He committed suicide in Berlin in 1945.

In an interview with *The Sun* newspaper (Saturday, August 13, 2011), a former Nigerian finance minister Olu Falae, recounted a brief history of Hitler's reason for his brutality.

> The First World War was a fight over the colonies by the major powers. It ended in 1918 with a treaty, where the allies—British, French, and Americans—defeated Germany and imposed a very one-sided onerous treaty on Germany, including the payment of reparation by the defeated to the victorious. But the one-sided nature of the treaty enabled Hitler to mobilize the German race and incite them to go into World War 11. He told the Germans that Germany

> has been enslaved. Not only did they lose a war, they are also being made to pay reparation to those who defeated them. That is the hallmark of slavery and Germany must fight to free herself from slavery. The World War 11 came because of that. More than 70 million people died in that war. But despite that huge loss of lives, it still ended at the negotiating table. We still had Nuremberg to bring that terrible carnage to a close.

There is no justification for the number of people who died in the hands of Hitler. However, the Western powers cannot, in conscience, completely extricate themselves from complicity in Hitler's evil regime. Hitler's claim that Germany was made to pay reparation after being defeated could not be wished away. In my opinion, those conditions that gave rise to Hitler's carnage are still rife in the present world: the rich getting richer at the expense of the less privileged. Hence, the Arab Spring and the *Occupy* projects had direct bearing on the same conditions that drove Hitler to war.

JOSEPH STALIN

Stalin is commonly described as one of the dreaded men of his generation. He was of a lowly birth, whose father was a cobbler. He graduated from being an underground Marxist to becoming a prominent member of the Communist Party.

Stalin was known for using and dumping or eliminating his fellow politicians. He formed an alliance with other members of the Politburo, who helped him defeat the left-wing opposition. He later turned against the right wing of the Communist Party and defeated them, thereby making himself the sole dictator of the Soviet Union by the early 1930s.

In the course of the years as a ruler, Stalin rounded up opponents and his own partners, forced them to confess to treason and executed them. These purges were extended to both civilians and the armed forces.

According to Hart, "Stalin's ruthless use of the secret police, and his program of arbitrary arrests and executions, and long terms in prison or labor camps for anyone even slightly critical of his rule, succeeded in cowing the population into submission" (1992, 330).

Stalin's thirst for blood was unleashed even on peasant farmers who resisted his unpopular policy of forced collectivization of agriculture. By Stalin's order, millions of the peasants were either killed or starved to death.

Stalin's hard-heartedness was prominent even with his family members. According to an account, "their only child, Jacob, was captured by the Germans in World War II. The Germans offered to exchange him, but Stalin turned the offer down, and Jacob died in a German prison camp" (1992, 333). He was at one point accused of having to do with the death of his second wife after his first died of tuberculosis.

Stalin's USSR conquered and annexed almost all the countries of Eastern Europe. Some put up resistance while others surrendered without a fight. Latvia, Lithuania, and Estonia were among Stalin's easy prey. Poland was shared between Stalin and Hitler.

It is estimated that in the course of his nearly twenty-five years as the ruler of Soviet Union, Stalin sent millions (about thirty million) of persons to their deaths, or to forced labor camps, or had them starved to death.

On the flip side, it is on record that everything about Stalin was not evil and destruction. The rapid industrialization of Soviet Union was attributable to Stalin's administration.

Again, during his lifetime, Stalin expanded the borders of the Soviet Union, set up a satellite empire in Eastern Europe, and transformed the USSR into a great power, with influence in every portion of the globe.

Another point worthy of note is that the Cold War was not solely blamed on Stalin. Western leaders had a share in the blame. However, it could be noted that the Cold War era commenced immediately after the World War II as a result of Stalin's expansionist policies and his implacable desire to spread the Communist system—and Soviet power—throughout the world.

Joseph Stalin, the seventy-three-year old dictator died in the Kremlin on March 5, 1953.

ADOLF HITLER AND JOSEPH STALIN

Adolf Hitler was to Germany what Joseph Stalin was to the Soviet Union. Like Hitler, who was originally born in Austria but later became a German, Stalin was born in Georgia in the Caucasus and later became the ruler of Soviet Union. Hitler and Stalin impacted world history and peoples' lives in many ways. They brought misery and sent many people to the great beyond. They also contributed to the economic buoyancy of Germany and Soviet Union, and by extension, to the various colonies annexed by the two most dreaded men in history.

Stalin and Hitler were contemporaries as well as partners in crime. They signed a non-aggression pact, but attacked Poland from the west and the east. Between Stalin and Hitler, it is difficult to determine who killed the most people. Both men intimidated and annexed other helpless small countries. Both men contributed a lot in the infrastructure and economic development of their countries and their colonies.

People make excuses for their action or inaction. Hitler and Stalin blamed certain segments of the society for their failure to safeguard the lives of their citizens. Hitler blamed Western powers for his commission of human atrocities. Stalin believed that the Western leaders were to blame for starting the Cold War. At the end of every stalemate between superpowers, the commoners are usually the losers.

If the West and Hitler and Stalin disagreed, none of the tripartite had anything to lose; rather the ordinary citizens lost both lives and property. Hitler took his own life. Stalin died, and his body preserved and placed in position of honor at the Red Square. Western powers are still flexing their muscles, intimidating countries, which disagree with them. But the souls of all those who died during the terror years of Stalin and Hitler are not resting in peace until there is justice in the world. It was the quest for peace and egalitarianism in the first place that gave rise to the Arab Spring agitation.

LEADERSHIP STYLES

Since the main issue of the Arab conflict is leadership, it would be worthwhile to discuss some notable *leadership styles*. In this regard, therefore, I will discuss the three leadership styles and my choice of participative leadership. My choice does not in any way make participative leadership the best style. It is rather based on the fact that participative leadership seems to be the norm all over the world. It is not perfect, but compared to autocratic and delegative leadership styles, participative is more widespread and tends to involve a larger representation of the populace.

Although the terms "participative" and "democratic" seem synonymous in principle, in practice they are worlds apart.

The reason I believe they are far apart is that many democratic systems are only democratic in name, every other aspect is either authoritarian or delegative. In the former, leaders make decisions independently with little or no input from the rest of the group. In the latter, leaders offer little or no guidance to group members and leave decision-making up to group members. While these are two extremes, participative lies in the middle.

If I were to choose, I would settle for the participative leadership style. In this leadership style, also known as the democratic leadership, "leaders offer guidance to group members, but they also participate in the group and allow input from other group members" (Cherry 2011). Participative leaders encourage group members to participate, but retain the final say over the decision-making process. Group members feel engaged in the process and are more motivated and creative. This is what makes the leadership style of democracy so proactive, because the leader is involved in almost every single aspect of governance. The leader may not be directly involved, but he/she is always at alert, in case he/she has to break the tie, by invoking the executive order.

The three arms might seem to operate independently, but in the end, the chief executive is the overall charge. There are, however, strict exceptions to the process. Though in charge, the chief executive carefully observes the rule of checks and balances. Otherwise, his/her arbitrariness might earn him/her an impeachment.

Although the participative style of leadership has all these lofty angles, it is also fraught with challenges. The autocratic leader gets things done and done fast, even if the people may not be happy about it.

The delegative leader is described as nonchalant and lackluster; at least the people are happy that they are delegated to run the affairs of the government. But in participative leadership, simple matters are overheated because everyone's opinion is considered.

For example, the government of the United States which runs a participative style wastes a lot of time arguing and debating over issues, to the detriment of the common good. A clear case is the debt ceiling debate by the United States Congress. The debate raged on for weeks, and was eventually agreed upon on the eve of the deadline. The casualty was the credit rating that was downgraded from triple A to double A+.

Plato had some reservation for democratic government after the government of Athens executed Socrates (1992, 213). It was not only Socrates who suffered at the altar of participative government. Manuel Noriega, Saddam Hussein, Robert Mugabe, et al, have either been eliminated, imprisoned, or hated in the name of promoting the participative ideals.

Nonetheless, irrespective of all of its negative aspects, participative is still considered the best of the three leadership styles because the interest of the majority is represented, or seemed to be represented.

Leadership is a charisma, which is not possessed by just any human being. Some are born into royalty, others acquire leadership skills. William and Harry, for instance, were not the only male children born in Britain, yet they automatically became princes by the simple reason that they were born the same year their mates were born, the only difference being that their parents are from the royal family.

Some people are better followers. They just are not disposed to the rigors of leadership. For such people, their interest is either not into leadership, or they are apathetic to leaders and resentful of the positions leaders occupy. History has shown that a society without a leader is a failed society. Somalia, for many years, was without a central leadership. This could lead to anarchy, and it did in Somalia when various factions were terrorizing people and taking hostage of citizens and tourists on land and on high seas. It has happened in many other societies across the globe. Those nations with a functional government still grapple with serious security challenges; imagine a nation without a central authority.

It is considered a patriotic duty for one to volunteer or be appointed or elected to lead. Imposition of a leader is not only immoral and unethical, it is also an insult on the people's intelligence, and therefore a quick way to commit political suicide. Most Arab countries and beyond have witnessed rulers staying in power till death did them part. So the Arab Spring was a way to remind other long term rulers to be prudent and leave when the ovation is loudest.

RELEVANT ASPECTS OF THE ARAB SPRING

ARAB SPRING AND TERRORISM

Thus far, popular revolution in the Arab world has claimed the leadership of three heads of state: Egypt, Tunisia, and Yemen. It has also cost the life of one head of state and ruler of Libya. The agitations and struggles are not showing any signs of abatement.

These governments believed that the agitators were terrorists, because they "terrorized" legally constituted governments. On the part of the agitators, they were simply reclaiming their mandate (if there was any in the first place) from *power usurpers*. They, therefore, believed that their action did not constitute terrorism.

Does every violent, anti-establishment protest constitute an act of terrorism? For instance, when Muslims in Palestine agitate for the creation of the Palestinian state and in the process take hostage of Jewish residents, are they engaging in terrorism? Again, when Catholics and Protestants clash in Northern Ireland, are they terrorizing anyone? When the Niger Delta militants take hostage of oil workers in Nigeria to demand an equitable distribution of oil wealth, are they rightly classified as terrorists?

These examples, almost all the time, involve lost of lives and destruction of state and individual properties. The perpetrators of these acts might describe themselves as "freedom fighters" or "liberators of the oppressed" or "individuals against injustice." On the other hand, government sources would like to classify them as "terrorists."

The credible argument against these agitators is that like in terrorism, the central issue involves some clandestine activities aimed mainly at an establishment. These activities are often deadly, while at other times, they could be just mere harassment of the civil populace in order to embarrass their government. Oftentimes, these individuals place unrealistic demands on the government. Like terrorists, some of these protesters are unidentifiable. Since no meaningful government will be willing to share power with a faceless group, government sources quickly tag such activities as terrorism, giving it a good reason to clamp down on them.

In recent years, the Nigerian government and a fanatical religious group known as Boko Haram have been having a running battle. This takes the form of destruction of lives and property, including bombing of worship places and other public buildings, including the United Nation's building in the capital city of Abuja.

The United States, after a prolonged consideration, finally declared this group a terrorist. The Nigerian government has tried in vain to identify the leaders of the group so that they could negotiate. The group claimed that it would only negotiate if the government could extend a similar amnesty as accorded the Niger Delta militants. Niger Delta militants started the whole idea of hostage taking in Nigeria. Their agitation was based on resource control of oil revenue from the region.

Boko Haram militants' claim of amnesty is based on the elimination of anything western, including western education. The Nigerian government has tried to exercise restraint due to the sensitive nature of issues bothering on religion. The unanswered question remains whether the two groups equally deserve any form of amnesty for breaching the peace and security of the country, an action which has been severally attributed to the offshoot of the Arab Spring.

THE ARAB SPRING AND POLITICAL PROPAGANDA

The press community as the fourth estate of government is as important as the government of the day. This means that the entire populace looks up to the media for not just information on government activities, but also for entertainment and unbiased situation reporting of events around the globe.

In the United States, for instance, some historical antecedents point to the fact that this whole idea of a press secretary is not as old as the United States government. "It was not until after President Abraham Lincoln's administration that Congress formally appropriated funds for a White House Staff, which at first consisted merely of a Secretary" (Dale 1998, 1).

Since the Press Department has come to be an integral part of the government, paid for by the American people, it is only expedient that the people expect the department to do a satisfactory and worthwhile job of information dissemination. But just as every other aspect of a democratic system, the press has, for the most part, been highly politicized.

Instead of political bickering and viewpoints, the press could devote time to enlighten the public regarding government's important decisions and policies as they affect the ordinary citizenry. This becomes necessary as Dr. Kendall Hope rightly observes:

> The time spent expressing partisan views is wasted time that could be spent educating our American public about many objective pieces of information that…include a better past and present coverage of the Iraqi culture and people.
>
> 2008, 27

Taking a cue from the American press, it is public that the various media houses have their own political biases and favorites. However, these partisan interests should be kept out of the press briefings by the chief press secretary of the White House. One way of keeping to the business of the day at such briefings is for the editors of these media houses to remind their reporters that press briefings are different from political meetings. The reporters should come to the briefing with a mind-set at the subject of the day and try to avoid questions, which clearly detract from the issue at stake.

Having said this, the blame does not lie squarely with the media houses. The White House press department should focus on issues aimed at just communicating the workings of the government, as opposed to comparing the present administration with any other administration. It is also not a forum for bolstering the ego of the president or of the ruling party. It must not be a forum to vilify other party interests and figures. Even in the event of out-of-context questions, the press secretary should show professionalism and control the flow in order to reduce or prevent frequent political vitriol associated with some media outfits.

The press secretary can use the press briefings to tell the American people the need to engage in those wars and steps taken by the government to bring the troops home safely with minimal casualty figures. It could also be an opportunity to reach out to the representatives of the Middle East countries in conflict to let them understand that America is not an occupying force. They should be made to understand the mission of America to these countries—mediation mission: mission that must be accomplished for peace to reign.

"Truth can be established through good investigative journalism and in-depth educational study and programming" (2008, 36). Investigative journalism is an aspect which has suffered neglect in some media houses. Some news networks are so sensationalized that one begins to wonder what the future holds for journalism.

As a news network, Fox News has won a large number of admirers. From a personal viewpoint, the same network is losing objective admirers through unbalanced and unfair reporting. As an influential TV station, the personal and collective views of its broadcasters and contributors used to be all-inclusive. But the dynamics gradually changed from popular programming to partisan bickering. Other stations probably engage in the same act, but are more subtle and sensitive.

If the media outlets should employ the same intensity with which they bicker in the dissemination of the truth of the Middle East conflict, the outcome of the conflicts might be different. The news media can take some time to express solidarity with families of veteran military men and women in conflict-ridden areas of the Middle East. The media can educate the Arab region regarding their relationship with the West. They can use their rich programming and wide audience to reach areas of the world that are ignorant of the main cause of tensions in the Middle East and to reassure the people of the region that a few bad elements in their society should not be a source of consternation between the West and the Arabs.

"Propaganda," according to Hope, "is the use of information to sway public opinion toward one person's or group's views" (2008, 29). The use of propaganda is immoral, unethical, unorthodox, irresponsible, and an expression of desperation and, to an extent, helplessness. It could be related to the proverbial drowning person reaching out to grab anything in his way to remain afloat.

The conflicts in the Middle East often reach fever pitch by the activities of propagandists. The insurgents use propaganda to either justify their cause or to advance their violent interests. For instance, during the uprising between the Egyptian government and the Muslim Brotherhood over the former president Morsi's detention, it was alleged that members of the Brotherhood inflated figures and made up stories to curry public sympathy. One such case was the use of fire extinguisher by the Brotherhood inside the mosque to paint a picture of government forces teargassing them.

To maintain a leading role in mediation efforts in the Middle East, the American Government press department, State Department, and indeed, American media outlets should have a leading role of either countering negative propaganda or correcting erroneous impressions by rebel and terrorist groups in the Middle East.

ARAB SPRING AND CONFLICT RESOLUTION PRACTICES

Conflict, crisis, intervention, management, prevention, and transformation are terms which often resonate in issues about the Middle East. Therefore, a definition of these terms will go a long way in helping to understand their place in mediation. Understanding these terms and their place in mediation is one instrument needed by any mediator in the Arab region to effectively mediate in conflicts in the area.

Conflict is defined as a state of open, often prolonged fighting: a battle or war. It is a state of disharmony between incompatible or antithetical persons, ideas, or interests: a clash. It could also be defined as a psychic struggle, often unconscious, resulting from the opposition or simultaneous functioning of mutually exclusive impulses, desires, or tendencies (*TheFreeDictionary*, 2012).

Crisis, on the other hand, is defined as a psychological or social condition characterized by unusual instability caused by excessive stress and either endangering or felt to endanger the continuity of an individual or group; especially: such a social condition requiring the transformation of cultural patterns and values (*Merriam-Webster Online Dictionary*, 2012).

"Crisis intervention refers to the methods used to offer immediate, short-term help to individuals who experience an event that produces emotional, mental, physical, and behavioral distress or problems" (Aguilera 1998). In international mediation, numerous examples abound. At the wake of the earthquake in Haiti, the United Nations dispatched humanitarian assistance to the crisis-stricken island in order to quell further crisis occasioned by the earthquake.

"Conflict management involves implementing strategies to limit the negative aspects of conflict and to increase the positive aspects of conflict at a level equal to or higher than where the conflict is taking place" (Rahim 2002, 208). In the days leading to the outbreak of civil war between Nigeria and Biafra, the Quakers employed international mediation, to avoid an escalation in an already volatile situation. (Bercovitch 2003, 200–201).

"Conflict prevention refers to a variety of activities aimed at anticipating and averting the outbreak of conflict" (Lund 2002). Diplomacy is one major tool in international mediation, which if properly applied could save a whole lot of problems. Successive American presidents have engaged in international mediation with leaders of Israel and Palestine in an effort to amicably settle their political differences.

Conflict transformation is the process by which conflicts are transformed into peaceful outcomes. It recognizes that contemporary conflicts require more than the reframing of positions and the identification of win-win outcomes. (Miall 2004, 4) The referendum, which gave rise to the "Good Friday Agreement" in Northern Ireland, was a result of a series of mediations involving almost every major country in Europe and beyond.

The tabulation below further explicates the terms for better understanding.

Conflict Management	Crisis Intervention	Conflict Prevention	Conflict Transformation
Power-sharing (e.g. Zimbabwe, where Robert Mugabe (ZANU Party) and Morgan Tsvangirai (MDC) share power. And in Kenya where Mwai Kibaki (PNU) and Raila Odinga (ODM) share political leadership).	Relief supplies (e.g. National Emergency Management Agency (NEMA and the United States government came to the aid of dwellers of New Orleans after horricane Katrina).	Peace-keeping mission. (e.g. Indian soldiers were mobilized to intervene in Somalia to avoid further breakdown of law and order).	Restorative justice/public hearings (e.g.Truth and Reconciliation Commission in South Africa after the apartheid regime).
Use of Force (e.g. NATO air strikes against Bosnian Serbs influenced the Dayton Accords). (Sisk 1996, 94).	Medical and food emergencies (e.g. The United Nations quickly sent much needed relief materials to Haiti after the massive earthquake, which destroyed the greater part of the country.)	Regional Organizations' mediation (e.g. Due to the election violence, the African Union sent delegation to Ivory Coast to find a way to mediate in the conflict).	Granting of Amnesty. (e.g. Amnesty granted by President Benigno Aquino III on alleged mutineers in the Philippines).
Economic Inducement (e.g. United States to Soviet Union).	Availability of world aid (e.g. Indonesia after tsunami).	Diplomatic summit (e.g. President Clinton's meeting with Israeli and Palestinian leaders at Camp Davis)	Referendum/ plebiscite. (e.g. "Good Friday Agreement" of Northern Ireland).

THE ARAB SPRING AND THE ISLAMIC FAITH

It would sound stereotypical to note that there seems to be a culture of violence associated with the Islamic religion. Controversial as this notation is, it is placed here as a scholarly topic to stimulate an academic discourse.

Islam is acclaimed a religion of peace. Therefore, it beats any enlightened imagination to note that a religion which is founded on peace would witness such spates of violence as seen in the present world events. In defense of the religion, just like every other organization infiltrated by fanatics—fanatics who wrongly interpret and implement certain injunctions, as they understand them, have infiltrated the Islamic religion. Otherwise, there is no meaningful, peaceful religion, which is expected to deliberately promote and encourage the same amount of violence noticed in areas of the world with a considerable number of Muslims.

There are indeed aspects of the Quran that are obviously excerpted out of context or without full context and used as justification for Holy War. One such misinterpreted sections of the Islamic Holy Book is as cited below.

> Fight against those who believe not in Allah, nor in the Last Day, nor forbid that which has been forbidden by Allah and His Messenger, and those who acknowledge not the religion of truth among the people of the Scripture, until they pay the Jizyah with willing submission, and feel themselves subdued.
>
> —Surah At-Taubah 9:29

A closer look at the above passage shows *Allah's messenger* as Prophet Mohammad. The *religion of truth* is Islam. *People of the scripture* in this context are probably Jews and Christians.

This aspect is often cited as justification for attacks on non-Muslim interests. At other times, fanatical preachers incite religious adherents to violence. For example, an influential Nigerian Islamic cleric, Sheik Ahmad Abubakar Gumi, at various times made inflammatory remarks capable of inciting fanatics against non-Muslims. He was once quoted as being in odds with the idea that there was a plot to oppress Muslims since the Chief of Army Staff is a non-Muslim (Enyiagu 2012, 1).

Any fanatic could capitalize on this statement to cause consternation among a hitherto peaceful government. Since Nigeria and Biafra fought a thirty-month bitter civil war, there has been a somewhat mutual distrust between people of various ethnic groups in the one united country. The army seems an exclusive preserve of the predominantly Muslim north. Army leadership has always come from the north. But for the first time, the leadership swings to a southern Christian.

Islam does not recognize a distinction between sacred and profane or between spiritual and temporal realms. Islam, therefore, molds the life of individuals and structures of a social order so that the kingdom of God may be promoted on earth. This could be cited as the reason behind the cleric's assertion. Because in a society where there is a clear demarcation between religion and politics, whoever becomes the army chief is immaterial. The constitution should be the reference point as opposed to any individual whims and caprices by either the head of state or an official of the state.

Prophet Mohammad founded Islam. As the founder of the movement, he obviously assumed the religious and political leadership known as the Caliph. In reality, therefore, "many Muslims argue that, unlike Christianity, Islam does not separate religion from state and a majority of Muslims around the world welcome a significant role for Islam in their countries' political life" (*LA Times*, December 5, 2010).

In Islam, the Fatherhood of God lays a foundation for Islamic Brotherhood. The Fatherhood of God is implemented by the ancestral fatherhood of Adam (Sura 4:11; 49:13). Islam also teaches that mankind was a single nation from the beginning. (Sura 2:213). Brotherhood has been made a supreme ideal and it has enabled Islam to reconcile elements of race, ethnicity, custom, and culture. As a result, brotherhood has been given due prominence in the interpersonal relationships.

Fanatics often misconstrue this aspect of the Islamic holy book to mean that everybody must belong to one religion, since mankind comes from one source and belong to one God. This oneness is superficial in application and only in principles. Every individual will never belong to one religion either by hook or crook.

Al-Qaida, described as a terrorist organization by the State Department, exists as a sub-cultural group in the Middle Eastern Islamic community. According to the group's founder, Usama bin Ladin, its main goal is to establish a pan-Islamic Caliphate throughout the world by working with allied Islamic extremist groups to overthrow regimes it deems *non-Islamic* and expelling Westerners and non-Muslims from Muslim countries (terrorismfiles.org, 2012).

Al-Qaida, since its establishment in the late 1980s, has increased in scope and strength. It was initially started to bring together Arabs who fought in Afghanistan against the Soviet invasion. In recent years, numerous terrorist acts have been directly or indirectly linked to it. The climax of which was the bombing of the World Trade Center in New York.

The allied military forces fighting in the Persian Gulf is not only confronted with faceless local militia, it also grapples with religious interest groups. Al-Qaida whose primary agenda is the protection of Islam feels violated and insulted because the *invading forces* have not operated according to the dictates of Islamic religion. The United Nations, on the other hand, steps up pressure to get the splinter groups to support the governments of the day to fight international terrorism. These divergent views give rise to lingering conflicts in some Arab countries. The result is that international efforts aimed at mediation in conflicts in these areas are stifled and almost impossible.

Throughout history, religion has inadvertently or deliberately lent itself to aggression, hostility, and brutality in order to remain relevant. Some of the reasons given for such hostility include heresy and apostasy by the so-called infidels. Jihads have been organized in the past to counter the infidels. At other times, crusades by other religions were organized for this same purpose.

As if religion has lost its original aim, its practitioners often tend to perpetrate all forms of social ills in the guise of religion.

In his discussion about the African predicament, George Ehusiani observes:

> In countries where religious clashes have not taken the dimension of a full-scale war there have been at least hundreds of lives lost to sporadic religious skirmishes. The result of all these is that human life is becoming increasingly cheaper by the day. Human blood is beginning to lose its traditional sacredness, because it is so frequently spilled for the flimsiest of reasons, while the awe traditionally associated with corpses is disappearing.
>
> —Ehusani 1991, 21

The constitution of most democratic governments clearly specifies a difference between religion and politics (Jefferson 1789). Till this day, this remains the charter governing most western governments. But this is not the same case with some Arab states. Therefore, any attempt by the West to intervene or mediate in conflicts in the Arab states is susceptible to suspicion of an imposition of democratic ideals.

To forestall this situation, Hope rightly cautioned:

> We imposed our own values upon the Iraqi people, hoping that giving them a democratically elected government would automatically stabilize their interactions. However, because they themselves did not directly seek this…they had no model to help them learn how to live in democracy.
>
> 2008, 51

One major flaw with this model is that this *strange system of government* would eventually be a sufficient reason to resort to violence in order to right the wrongs or as Hope puts it, "to make things feel *normal* again."

No matter how much western countries try to play religious neutrality—that is the claim of secularism—they cannot deny the high prevalence of Christianity in their mediation efforts in the Middle East.

This being the case, therefore, it would be practically impossible for the international community to successfully mediate in the conflicts in the Middle East. "Middle Eastern people, to a large extent, think collectively about issues that challenge their culture. They often make decisions based on… what their local mosque dictates…" (2008, 49).

Sharia regulates all religious and social affairs. Islamic legislations cover all aspects of human affairs: food, drinks, intoxicants, meat, dress, business, inheritance, administration, etcetera.

In Islam, a religious heretic or rebel risks execution, crucifixion, or maiming of some organs of the body or be exiled (Sura 5:36). For a thief, the punishment is the chopping off of the hand (Sura 5:41).

Sura 2:178 stipulates thus:

> In the cases of murder, the free for the free,
> The slave for the slave,
> The woman for the woman…

This is known in Islam as the law of equality, because criminals are punished according to the Koranic law of retaliation.

Note that in Islam a political role is religious obligation. This is the reason every political office holder must have an adequate knowledge of Islamic laws.

To therefore plan any meaningful mediation in conflicts in the Arab world, prominence must be given to the Islamic religion and its operations. Transfer of values should by all means be avoided, realizing that what works in a secular state may not work in a strictly Islamic setting.

ARAB SPRING AND CULTURAL TYPES IN MEDIATION

Personality traits, cultural differences, environmental influences, temperaments, and a host of other conditions are among the factors influencing dialogue and mediation, especially in the culturally diverse Middle Eastern region.

One way of understanding the recurrent conflicts, which finally gave rise to the Arab Spring, is to examine the various cultures of the world. It is also this diversity in cultures that seems to be the bane of a lasting peace in the world. While one region employs a certain approach to a problem, the other wants it the other way around, both justifiably rationalizing their approach.

WESTERN

> Pragmatism is the predominant characteristic of American business culture. Business relationships are nurtured by their potential for profitability and trust is often found in the terms of a binding contract. Trust, or lack thereof, profoundly influences American negotiation practices. American businesspersons prefer a straightforward dialog where needs and concerns are addressed somewhat candidly. Through a position of strength and openness each side works to make concessions until a mutually beneficial agreement can be reached. This willingness to make concessions is motivated by pragmatism—the willingness to avoid unnecessary time and expense.
>
> —Sgubini, Norman

SOUTH AND CENTRAL AMERICAN

> Brazilians are known for being warm and friendly people in personal life and in business relations. Unfortunately, such conduct may create an informal negotiation environment that may not please negotiators from other cultures. Many business people characterize the way Brazilians negotiate as somewhat informal. Nonetheless, some other values come in place when they are negotiating.

Regarding these values, Brazilians ranked honesty, trustworthiness and ethics as being essential during the negotiation process. Transparency and punctuality are also important factors in order to show a party is acting in good faith and is trustworthy. Finally, it is important to build a business relationship before starting a negotiation, this way the parties will try to communicate to each other the image of an honest, trustworthy and ethical person, able to duly carry on a successful negotiation.

—Potenza, Sgubini

CENTRAL EUROPEAN

Credibility and social reputation when dealing with Italian businesses are decisive factors for successful negotiations. Generally, business people in Italy prefer to negotiate and maintain a business relationship with an executive or manager of a firm. Elegance and appearance are important considerations in Italian culture. More so than in many other countries an attractive, well-dressed individual is considered more reliable. Italians prefer to take their time negotiating and be familiar with who they're talking to. Indeed, being in a rush to sign an agreement will lead to unfulfilled expectations. For example, during a business lunch it is important to begin with relaxed conversation; giving your partner the opportunity of enjoying lunch before you get to the subject you're interested in.

—Sgubini, Cardinale

EASTERN EUROPEAN

> Negotiations with Russians often involve flared tempers. During negotiations and meetings, temper tantrums and walkouts often occur. As a foreigner, you are expected to be on time to all business appointments. However, your Russian counterpart may be late, as this may be a test of your patience. Do not expect an apology from a late Russian, and do not demonstrate any kind of attitude if your business appointments begin one or two hours late. This may also be a test of your patience. Do not show the soles of your shoes, as this is considered impolite. They are considered dirty, and should never come in contact with any type of seat. Be alert and open to taking a drink or having a toast, as refusing to do so is a serious breach of etiquette. Speaking or laughing loudly in public is considered rude, as Russians are generally reserved and somber.
>
> —Hofstede, Priest

MIDDLE EASTERN

Religion plays a very important role in most of the countries of the Middle East. The predominant religion for the Arab and Middle Eastern countries is Islam. Muslims follow the doctrines of the Koran. The entire lifestyle of the Middle Easterners is highly influenced by their religion. This is an important piece of information which a negotiator to the region must know.

AFRICAN

> Though their life is hard, the Amhara of Ethiopia are a proud people, proud of their ethnicity, religion and their special place in the world. Their culture is strong, developed over many centuries, and it has withstood the incursions of outside governments and religions.
>
> —Bender 1971

From this quotation, it is understood that the Amharas can do all it takes to protect their pride. A mediator who is not originally from the region must acquaint himself or herself with the sensitivity of the people and treat them accordingly.

ASIAN

Asians place a great deal of importance on relationships. The building of long lasting relationships is tantamount for business success in Asia. The concept of "saving face" is inherent in this region. Asians will go to great lengths to save face and avoid embarrassment. The loss of face is not easily forgotten nor is it easily forgiven. Do not use large hand movements. The Chinese do not speak with their hands. Your movements may be distracting to your host. Do not point when speaking. Bowing or nodding is the common greeting; however, you may be offered a handshake. Wait for the Chinese to offer their hand first. Allow the Chinese to leave a meeting first (Hofstede, Priest).

These are facts, which can aid a mediator from another cultural region to have a successful session in the Asian culture.

MEDIATION TYPES AND SPECIFIC CULTURES

Cultural Type:	Challenge to Mediation:	Mediation Type that May Work Best:
Western (Christianity)	Presumed Pragmatism—Mediation could be stalled when it is assumed that each session must produce a quick result.	Workplace Mediation
South and Central American (Christianity)	Informal Negotiating Environment—Mediation is a serious business, which certainly demands a serious setting. This culture seems to over-simplify mediation.	Interpersonal Mediation
Central European (Christianity)	Preference to negotiate with an executive over a delegate—In this regard, mediation could suffer a serious setback in the absence of an authority figure as opposed to an intelligent mediator who is not an executive.	Landlord/Tenant Mediation
Eastern European (Orthodox)	Temper tantrums—Tantrums are bound to flare up in negotiations, but incessant temper tantrums could hinder mediation.	School or family Mediation

Middle Eastern (Islam)	Religious inclination—It is believed that everything in Islamic culture is governed by religion. Since different interest groups could engage in mediation, would they be accommodated?	Nonprofit Organizations and Community-based Mediation
African (Animism)	Over Protection of cultural identity—Cultural identity is the pride of a people. But in mediation, the disputants might focus on culture, to the detriment of the main cause of crisis, thereby defeating the purpose of mediation.	Environmental and property ownership Mediation
Asian (Buddhism)	No use of hand gestures—For a mediator coming from the West, this could be a challenge, in the sense that most westerners buttress points by hand gesticulations.	Discrimination and racially charged Mediation

PROSPECTS OF PEACE IN THE ARAB REGION

According to the Christian holy books,

> There is a time for everything, and a season for every activity under the heavens: 2 a time to be born and a time to die, a time to plant and a time to uproot, 3 a time to kill and a time to heal, a time to tear down and a time to build, 4 a time to weep and a time to laugh, a time to mourn and a time to dance, 5 a time to scatter stones and a time to gather them, a time to embrace and a time to refrain from embracing, 6 a time to search and a time to give up, a time to keep and a time to throw away, 7 a time to tear and a time to mend, a time to be silent and a time to speak, 8 a time to love and a time to hate, a time for war and a time for peace.
>
> Ecclesiastes 3:1–8, (NIV)

This quote seems to sum up the activities around the present-day Middle East and the Arab region. At one point in history, the Middle Eastern region was classified the cradle of civilization. Meaning that the present-day so-called superpowers and first worlds copied or emerged from the region. As generations passed, the region became a harbinger of violence, religious plurality, and all sorts of anti civilizing activities, including in recent years, the Gulf War. It was the Gulf War that caused the most devastating effect in the lives and well-being of the people of the once historic region. As the region that produced notable historic figures—including Jesus Christ and Prophet Mohammed, one would expect that the region would be as peaceful as paradise. This expectation seems a far cry.

Rebuilding the infrastructure is one thing; to rebuild a devastated humanity is a huge project, which may never be achieved. This last clause is certainly debatable. Nonetheless, it begs the question to say that human life is not ever revamped. This means that the only one who has risen from the dead was Jesus Christ. Every other dead is dead for good. Even when individuals claim to rise from the dead, usually for medical reasons, they hardly live long thereafter. So only American magicians can tell us how best to resurrect all the innocent men, women, children, and ordinary Iraqis killed in that senseless war. "Such a sad reality. I feel sick to my heart with every passing day that it continues—all of the violence in the Middle East specifically—because it is truly a unique geographic and cultural microcosm of violence" (Hope 2012).

In rebuilding the Middle East, the international community in collaboration with Arab leaders should first employ the services of professional mediators to calm frayed nerves in the region. This becomes necessary because it could be an exercise in futility to build the bricks without first building the body and mind of the intended brick dweller.

In this context, therefore, the role of the professional mediators would be to get the various interest and splinter groups to present their grievances with a view to discussing them at the highest places. This will also be an opportunity for the coalition forces to admit their mistakes and be humble about it. It is in corroboration of Dr. Mary Kendall Hope (2008): "One of our basics of fair and respectful interactions from one person or group of people to another is acknowledging when one or a group has done something wrong and very sincerely apologizing for it" (2008, 67).

As part of the rebuilding project, a team of professional counselors should be engaged. Their role would be to reach out to the warring factions and their leadership and to get them understand that there is more to life than just incessant warfare. Since it is not possible to round off all the militia to counsel them, a national reorientation project will surely work. This will serve as a teachable moment for the Iraqis in order to forestall negative indoctrination. "To not provide them education about the American people will allow the same forces within the Iraqi culture who are educating them falsely, to continue to indoctrinate them falsely about our intentions" (2008, 76).

It is only when these individuals have tapped into a certain level of conscientiousness, which enables them to respect life and property, that any meaningful infrastructure rebuilding and lasting peace will succeed. Yes, respect life and through empathizing with the same feelings present in others and opposite feelings/beliefs...to exist. These are indeed high goals as compared to the present "norm" in the Middle Eastern culture in many "fundamental/terrorist" type subcultures within this region and within the Islamic faith that it is built on (Hope 2012).

To talk of peace, justice must be present; otherwise, it becomes a charade, a mere exercise in futility and a clear possible obstacle to progress.

The incessant wars and violent elimination of notable personalities of the region remains a big obstacle to peace in the area. For instance, the entire invasion of Iraq was a regrettable mistake. But the most tragic aspect of that invasion was the culmination of the hanging of Saddam Hussein. Until this generation of Iraqis passes, the mark left by his death remains indelible. He had loyalists and relatives who felt betrayed by other segments of Iraq. He had soldiers and other security experts who were happier under his regime. These people might want to avenge the death of their mentor and hero in any way, shape, or form.

Lack of trust is another reason why it is difficult to accomplish any meaningful rebuilding of relationships in the Arab region. An average Arab citizen views Western activities with suspicion. In the same vein, the West approaches the Arab with a good amount of caution. Arabs believe that the West are out to pillory their rich cultural heritage and plunder their natural resources. The West see most Arabs as out to harm every westerner in their view.

Insofar as there is mutual distrust among the groups, any meaningful relationship rebuilding is a far cry and difficult to attain.

Economic factors pose yet another major obstacle to the rebuilding of relationships in the region. The world economy plummets in recent years. To start a reasonable rebuilding of relationships, words of mouth are not just enough. The international community can extend a hand of friendship to the people of the region by engaging in several works of charity to the people who have been impoverished by wars and violence. "If already committed funds were reallocated from simple military force TO a better representation of ambassadors or emissaries I believe this would begin a path toward a better use of the investment of US money and energy—IF a force of belief and power among the American people were behind it" (Hope 2012).

Politics is one issue, which may not be easily wished away in an effort to rebuild relationships in the region. Each successive government has its own agenda and areas of interest. It is the Democrats today; it might be the Republicans tomorrow. Each of the parties has various policies regarding how to deal with issues of foreign relations.

It is being suggested that the onus of *conscience* is on the United States to rebuild Iraq as much as possible without any conditions and strings because they took their war to Iraq. Iraq did not wage war against America. Since the war was not justified in the first place, America owes it to the people of Iraq to return their country to the same shape they found it. This is a Herculean task, which will not be attainable. But it does not hurt to try for the sake of justice and fairness.

It is not that difficult to begin to understand cultural and sub-cultural differences, needs for respect, utilizing the language and culture to foster peace. These are truly reachable goals if those in power will simply embrace the validity of conflict resolution and education in cultural interactions and respect to work. "It would work. If implemented with patience and caring, it would be amazing how much things could change toward peace in time" (Hope 2012).

Most fairy tales end with "they lived happy ever after." However, war tones are different. How I wish war stories could be told with the same ending. Wars and their attendant devastation never end happily, irrespective of the victor or the vanquished. The victor, even when he gloats in his gallantry, lives with guilt ever after. The vanquished laments in regret, shame, and humiliation all the days of his life.

For academic purposes, a hypothetically peaceful Middle East would be so nice that the region could compete with the rest of the prosperous countries in terms of economic and sociological prosperity. I have in all my adult life been an eternal optimist. This optimism has carried me beyond my immediate frustrations and trials. It is this same sense of optimism which makes me believe that there is hope for a lasting peace in the volatile Middle East.

Apart from competing with other developed worlds in economic and sociological prosperity, a peaceful Middle East would certainly focus on returning to its historic glorious days, when the world recognized the region as a cradle of civilization. This recognition would in turn bolster the tourism potentials of the Persian Gulf states.

A peaceful Middle East would focus more on religious liberalization, in which every individual would be free to worship his God according to the dictates of his conscience and choosing, rather than one based on family and tribal tradition of one religion for all.

A peaceful Middle East would educate its citizens, and by so doing defeat superstition, which has been the bane of progress and development in the region.

As a region surrounded by arid deserts, artificial boundaries may not be easily delineated. However, there are ethnic and religious boundaries which could form natural borders. For instance, all language, ethnic and religious groupings could have their different nation states. When the nations speak one language, understand each other's cultural sensitivities, they tend to live in peace with each other.

Judging by the ethnic and cultural tensions and diversity amongst the dwellers of the Middle East, representative democratic form of government would be ideal for the region.

"*Representative* democracy is a form of democracy in which citizens allow others—usually elected officials—to represent them in government processes and are not necessarily directly involved in any of the processes of legislation or lawmaking" (Conjecture Corporation, 2003–2012). They need to create their own name for it—to own it—as to make it their own satisfies an important need in this region. When they "own" their own solution and it is not given or forced on them, they will work to keep it. I believe this is a central point for a workable option toward peace for the Middle East. "It must be religious liberation (our term) but defined in their own terms and specifics in every way and be incorporated into their governmental structure as well" (Hope 2012).

Some of the nations of the region base their governments on the monarchical or theocratic systems. Even when they have a representative structure or the democratic constitution, some still base their government on family succession. For instance, in Syria, the current president who is the son of the former president came into office due to his father's position. "The Syrian Parliament has unanimously approved the nomination of the late president Hafiz al-Assad's son, Dr. Bashar al-Assad, to become the 16th President of the Syrian Arab Republic" (café-Syria.com. Retrieved 02/2012).

The popular understanding in Iraq was that Saddam Hussein was grooming one of his sons to succeed him. That chapter ended with the coalition invasion and the subsequent death of the president and his two sons.

In Iran, for instance, "At the top of Iran's power structure is the Supreme Leader, Ayatollah Ali Khamenei, who succeeded Ayatollah Ruhollah Khomeini, the father of the Iranian Revolution…" (Iran Chamber Society, 2001–2012).

The Kurds in Iraq and Kuwait could combine to ask for nationhood, if that is a panacea for peaceful coexistence in the region. Same goes for the Arabs in both countries.

If the people of the region are happier splintering into religious groups, the Shiites are large enough to form a government. The Sunnis are equally large to seek statehood. These groups can appoint, elect, or select their own people to represent and govern them.

The West therefore, has no business meddling in the affairs of a people who have internally decided on what structure of government that is workable for them. If the region were left alone to manage their own affairs, there would be relative peace and tranquility in the region and the world over. Just as Dr. Hope rightly asserts: "We continue to try and make them play by our rules, and lives continue to be lost while we spin our wheels doing this" (2008, 103).

In the course of my outpatient nursing clinics, I have encountered adults who would almost cry at the sight of me wearing a lab coat. If they get through that first stage of fear and anxiety, they usually turn around and exhale with a sense of relief that the procedure was not as bad as expected. It is not usually my presence that creates the anxiety; it is the fact that my lab coat reminds them of their childhood experience whereby their parents took them to a doctor wearing a lab coat, holding a needle, which inflicted pain.

"For the people of Iraq, the mere sight of a uniform stimulates many more feelings of terror and expectation than Americans can begin to imagine" (Hope 2008, 107). In this regard, therefore, a proper approach would be to separate operations according to their volatility or otherwise. What this means is that civilians whose mission is nothing but charity should cover areas where locals need food, water, and medicine. For the most part, insurgents do not target charity workers, whether they are soldiers or civilians, insofar as they are dressed like everyone around—not in rags, though.

As for soldiers who battle terrorists on a daily basis, wearing of uniform may not only help them to execute their mission properly, it would also enable them to recognize each other as soldiers as different from militants.

In terms of the emissaries and diplomats to the region, they should identify with the culture of the people and dress appropriately. If the secretary of state were to meet with the emir of Baghdad (as an example), though she is American and represents American interest, dressing like an average Iraqi woman for just that purpose would not make her less of a secretary or American.

Dressing like the people is a way of identifying with them. By identifying with them, there is less tension and suspicion by the people. This is where relationships begin to heal, and the people begin to develop trust in the American mission in the region.

CONCLUSION

Algeria, Bahrain, Comoros, Djibouti, Egypt, Iran, Iraq, Israel, Jordan, Kuwait, Lebanon, Libya, Mauritania, Morocco, Oman, Palestinian territories, Qatar, Saudi Arabia, Somalia, Sudan, Syria, Tunisia, United Arab Emirates, Yemen are the countries located within a geographical and cultural zone known as the Arab world or the Middle East. While peace and stability have become a rare commodity allover the world, some of the countries mentioned here seem to have a fair share of restiveness.

It sounds like an irony of life that God's own land, of all places on earth, refuses to know peace, irrespective of numerous efforts at peaceful resolution of conflicts in the Middle East. As the region that produced notable historic figures—including Jesus Christ and Prophet Mohammed, one would expect that the region would be so peaceful and habitable. So far, the opposite seems to be the case.

Scholars and interested individuals have sometimes believed that this was a curse brought upon the region by their ancestors. They relate it to activities surrounding the unjust crucifixion of one of their sons. It should be recalled that after Pontius Pilate washed his hands clean of any complicity in the death of Jesus Christ, the Jews did not mince words to declare, "Let his blood be on us and our children" (NJB Matt. 27:25). Jews are not, strictly speaking, Arabs; however, territorially, the Arab Spring took place in their region.

Some of the salient issues discussed in this paper are recurrent and controversial in nature. They recur in the sense that peace talks have been ongoing and broken for years on end. The topics are controversial because Western involvement, which was originally designed to be a solution, has not really attained that purpose. Some of those aspects worthy of note are as itemized and discussed herein.

Prior to the advent of the Arab Spring, the Middle East had known and endured rulers who ruled the people in the same fashion as the ancient Pharaohs. One of those modern day pharaohs was Saddam Hussein, whose government was somewhat ruthless. He flaunted his wealth and demonstrated that power rested in him and his cohorts. Like everything, which had a beginning and an end, Saddam rose, reigned, and fell. While many applauded his fall, the manner of that fall leaves an indelible and regrettable mark in the land of the ancient Mesopotamia till date. Saddam and his sons were killed, a situation which further fueled the simmering conflicts even beyond Iraq. That was a case of mediation gone wrong.

What I believe would have happened in Iraq would have been for the United States government and its allies to focus more on building a bridge to let Saddam give up some or all of his political powers, while wielding the option of war as the Best Alternative to a Negotiated Agreement (BATNA).

BATNA refers to the course of action that will be taken by a party engaged in negotiations if the talks fail and no agreement can be reached. Having a good BATNA can help you negotiate on the merits. Rather than stubbornly clinging to one's position, a good negotiator, equipped with a powerful BATNA, recognizes when to make compromises in order to arrive at a negotiated and binding agreement. One who has a better and stronger BATNA usually presents the matter and discusses it according to its own merit. This principle saves both time and effort, and gives rise to a much-needed agreement. Developing a good BATNA not only enables one to determine what is a minimally acceptable agreement, it will probably raise the minimum (Ury 1991, 106).

At no epoch has war been of any benefit to anyone. The government, the soldiers, and the civil populace have a lot to lose in a war situation. For instance, after the war in Iraq, the devastation was so enormous that the United States and the Iraqi government joined forces to rebuild the once beautiful city of Baghdad and for the most part, other cities in Iraq. They may rebuild the infrastructure as much as possible, but the human toll can never be the same again.

In this light, therefore, the United States government can save face by looking for a way to get the Arab world understand that the crisis in the Middle East is not a show of Western military might, but rather a service to an oppressed populace. This can be achieved by empowering the locals to confront their own issues by talking with the various interest groups with a view to address their own concerns and grievances, and to formulate their own mutual agreement.

By so doing, western countries can demonstrate a good measure of transparency in mediating in conflicts in the Middle East. This will go a long way in correcting the notion that seems to suggest that Western intervention in the region was aimed at protecting western interests. For instance, it was widely believed that the United States took the war to the Persian Gulf in order to deal with the terrorists over there and protect lives and property in the United States. "Laudable as the policy might sound, the ideal thing would have been to formulate strategies in Iraq toward goals that will serve the needs of the Iraqi people, instead of *our interpretation* of what they need…" (Hope 2008, 5).

The situation that gave rise to the Arab Spring did not just happen in one day; it was a series of events perpetrated by the same set of rulers who lorded it over the people for as long as it lasted. When the people spoke in one voice, they confronted the status quo. The resultant effect was the dismantling of governments which were hitherto untouchable. That was a lesson in governance which sent shivers to the entire Arab region and the rest of the world. Perpetuity in government as well as taking the citizenry for granted was checkmated. The Arab Spring protesters reclaimed freedom of expression and of association.

Mediation is a serious business as well as a sensitive one. Therefore, if the setting is wrongly chosen and/or arranged, the outcome might be counterproductive. The Arab Spring and its attendant transition bottleneck could have been averted if mediators took thorough consideration of the vastness and the diverse nature of the Arab region. The physical setting could have an impact on facilitating communication, gaining control of the argument, reducing or increasing pressure on the parties, and insuring the safety of all those involved (Chan, Leviton, Greenstone).

Neutrality of venue and mediators cannot be overemphasized for the success of mediation in the Arab region. Privacy, security, accessibility are some of the factors to consider in mediation in the Arab region. It is also important that the disputants must feel equally empowered. (Chan 2007, 11–12).

The general rule for mediation setting, whether in the Arab world or in interpersonal disputes include the following:

- Everyone should be able to see and hear everyone else and participate easily in discussions.
- Members of one party should be able to sit together if they choose. Couples typically want to sit side by side.
- Everyone should be physically comfortable, undistracted, and feel as safe as possible.
- The mediators should be able to control the process.
- The setting should suggest mediator impartiality.
- Pick a location that feels comfortable and private: not too large, not too dim or cluttered.
- The suitable furniture for mediation is a round table or a square table, or a rectangular table. The sitting arrangement is strictly important.

—Beer, Steief 1997, 28

A conflict, which was as convoluted as the Arab Spring would require seasoned and experienced mediators, who possess certain natural qualities not taught or learned in school. Appropriate mediators should possess intelligence, tact, drafting skills, a sense of humor, and have specific knowledge and expertise of the conflict at hand. Mediators who possess these attributes are likely to be acceptable to all sides in a conflict, and consequently enhance the parties' motivation to reach a peaceful settlement (Bercovitch 2003, 20).

Arab Spring cuts across various spectra of life. Therefore, for the mediator, whether he or she is religious or animist is irrelevant. Whether he is black or white has no place.

Nonetheless, certain qualities remain non-negotiable. Apart from being and remaining neutral, he or she must be talented. The talent is reflected in the sensitivity with which the mediator listens, hears, responds, empathizes, creates, draws parties into the process and deftly maneuvers through the delicate and difficult moments with an intuitive sense of timing and appropriateness. The following roles are also expected of an Arab Spring mediator: process facilitator, discussion facilitator, clarifier, idea generator, face-saver, agent of reality, messenger, distinguisher of needs from wants, and trainer (Chan, Leviton, Greenstone).

Mediation in the Arab region requires tact and orderliness. Therefore, the four stages of mediation must be followed.

1. Opening Statement

   The mediator discusses the process and describes the mediator's role, the roles of the participants, and the general expectations for the mediation. The purposes of the opening statement include the following:

   - Establish a safe environment to negotiate.
   - Establish the mediator's credibility and control of the proceedings.
   - Explain the mediation process and what will be asked of the parties.
   - Obtain necessary commitments from the parties concerning their involvement.
   - Be sensitive to concerns raised by the parties.

   —Chan 2007, 18

Before the actual commencement of mediation, the mediator must assure the disputants of his/her neutrality. The disputants must make a commitment to respect each other's time and values. Expectations are also pointed out to the parties in regard to their commitment to the time required for resolving the issues, after which they are requested to provide their consent to commence the process (Chan 2007, 18–19).

2. Information Sharing and Issue Identification

- Ask each disputant to state his/her perception of the conflict. Hear all evidence pertinent to the dispute. Collect any evidence relating to the dispute, such as written contracts, cancelled checks, receipts, and reports.
- Clarify issues.
- Clarify remaining differences and see whether the disputants can form a common understanding.
- Listen actively to the disputants' issues and feelings as they are talking:
- Learn about the parties' interests and priorities.
- Determine whether the parties agree on the credibility of the incidents and information.
- Clarify the differences and see whether the parties can form a common understanding.
- Formulate clear goals.
- Attempt to settle simple issues. Build on success.
- Note parties' underlying needs and hopes. These are at the core of the dispute. Having them addressed and met will be the core of a resolution.

—Chan, Leviton, Greenstone

3. Exchange and Negotiation

This stage encompasses problem solving, but not limited to it. At this stage, parties

- identify and evaluate a range of ideas,
- negotiate with everyone's interests in mind,
- develop and test specific proposals, and

- gain confidence in their ability to resolve the situation and to build commitment to the emerging agreement.

—Chan, Beer, Stief

4. Agreement and Conclusion

   The following are the elements that an agreement should contain.

   - Details specifics: who, what, when.
   - Is evenhanded and not conditional.
   - Uses clear, familiar wording.
   - Emphasizes positive action.
   - Deals with any pending proceedings.
   - Provides for the future.

—Chan, Beer, Stief

It is not just sufficient to apply the above conditions and stop at that. Successful mediation in the Middle East and the entire Arab region should be able to identify a particular style of mediation and work toward achieving success in it.

The four mediator styles are: facilitative mediation, transformative mediation, evaluative mediation, restorative justice mediation. The first three were the original styles of mediation. Restorative justice later became part of the group; it is described as "a systematic response to wrongdoing that emphasizes healing the wounds of victims, offenders and communities caused or revealed by the criminal behavior" (Chan 2007, 29).

The main point in restorative justice mediation is identifying and taking steps to repair harm. Another focal point here is to identify the nature and extent of the victim's loss and to explore how the offender might begin to repair the harm caused by the criminal act. Yet another important aspect is that agreements are made concerning restitution schedules, follow-up meetings and monitoring procedures (Chan, VanNess, Strong).

Facilitative is the foremost style of mediation. In facilitative mediation, the mediator structures a process to assist the parties in reaching a mutually agreeable resolution. One advantage of this style is that it empowers parties to take responsibility for their own disputes and the resolution of the disputes. The flip side of this style is that mediation takes too long, and too often ends without agreement (Zumeta, Chan).

Transformative mediation has similar advantages and disadvantages as facilitative mediation. Supporters of transformative mediation worry that outcomes can be contrary to standards of fairness and that mediators in these approaches cannot protect the weaker party. The distinctive points of transformative mediation are: transformative mediators leave responsibility for the outcomes with the parties; transformative mediators feel (and express) a sense of success when empowerment and recognition occur, even in small degrees; they do not see a lack of settlement as a failure (Zumeta, Chan, Spangler, Bush, Folger).

In evaluative mediation, the mediator controls the process and suggests solutions for resolving the conflict. The focus of an evaluative mediation is primarily upon settlement. The mediators will make their best efforts to get the parties to compromise, if necessary, to achieve a result (Chan, Zumeta).

Sometimes, the problem lies with the individuals who try to prove stubborn in mediation. At such times, a couple of strategies could be of assistance. If in the course of negotiation the parties refuse to play or deliberately employ some deceptive dirty tricks, the negotiation process might be jeopardized if not handled properly.

There are a couple of ways to get reluctant players to participate in negotiation. You may yourself concentrate on the merits, rather than on position. In effect, you can change the game simply by starting a new one (Ury 1991, 107). He lists some of the methods as: Principled Negotiation, Negotiation Jujitsu, and One-Text Procedure.

Of all the methods propounded by the book, *one-text procedure*, for me, remains a formidable force to getting the other party to participate effectively in reaching a negotiated settlement. The unique thing about this process is that through the instrumentality of a third party, a number of puzzles could be solved. For example, a third party can often suggest some impartial basis for resolving differences. He can separate the people from the problem and direct the discussion to interests and options.

In my opinion, *one-text procedure* is comparable to *shuttle diplomacy* in mediation. In *one-text procedure,* even if the other side is not willing to talk to you directly (or vice versa), a third party can take a draft around (Ury 1991, 116). In *shuttle diplomacy*, the mediator practically oscillates between the disputants.

In addition, the other party might misrepresent facts and figures. The wise thing to do is to separate the people from the problem. Not to take them for their word, unless absolutely convinced of their claim. It is also wise to express it if the physical surroundings seem to be prejudicial (Ury 1991, 132).

There is a natural inclination for people to defend their claims and beliefs, irrespective of whatever any other party says, thinks, or believes. However, there comes a point when someone has to yield to the other for peaceful and harmonious coexistence. This is a case where *positional bargaining* is shelved.

Positional bargaining therefore is a situation whereby people in a dispute stick to their own side of the story with little or no interest in, or consideration for the other party's storyline. Each of the parties argues only to defend their position with some concession just for the purpose of reaching a compromise. Studies have proven that such agreements attained through positional bargaining are so ephemeral, unreliable, unwise, inefficient, a waste of time, and therefore, one easy way to lose face in relationships. As more attention is paid to positions, less attention is devoted to the underlying concerns of the parties (Fisher, Patton, Ury).

The flip side of the futility of positional bargaining is what the Harvard Negotiation Project called *principled negotiation* or *negotiation on the merits*. The method is summarized as follows:

1. People: separate the people from the problem.
2. Interests: focus on interests, not positions.
3. Options: generate a variety of possibilities before deciding what to do.
4. Criteria: insist that the result be based on some objective standard.

In contrast to positional bargaining, the principled negotiation method of focusing on basic interests, mutually satisfying options, and fair standards typically results in a *wise* agreement" (Ury 1991, 14).

It is absolutely important to note that it takes skill, intelligence, and astuteness to be able to counter tricks and innuendos emitting from the opponent's camp. It is only he who is able to decipher the other party's mind-set that succeeds in reaching a negotiated and possibly lasting agreement.

My assessment of this work is that it has only scratched the surface of the complex issues in a complex region of the world—the Middle East and the entire Arab states. I make this assessment with the same humility which propelled Thomas Aquinas to conclude, "All that I have written seems to me like straw compared to what has now been revealed to me" (Holt 2008, 1). However, given the scope of the work, I believe I have done a great job in stimulating academic discussions on the subject of the Persian Gulf region. The book is by no means an exhaustive discussion on the subject. It rather exposes new vistas for the international community to address local issues in the Middle East and elsewhere in the civil society.

We may not all live in the Arab world, but as a global village, an upheaval in one region of the world affects all other regions. The entire world should not fold their arms and wait for Arabs to resolve their own conflicts. The United Nations and other meaningful and peace-loving nations must step in and facilitate conflict resolution efforts in the region.

The ripple effects of wars and conflicts have no boundaries. For instance, the civil war between Nigeria and Biafra caused the influx of refugees in Gabon. The Liberian war caused a huge immigration of refugees in Nigeria. Currently, the conflicts in Syria are the major reason Turkey is saturated with fleeing Syrians. Conflicts in the Middle East could and have sent energy costs skyrocketing in major consumer nations.

Therefore, the whole human race must come together to mediate in conflicts before they escalate. And it is these mediation efforts that give rise to peaceful political transition in the Arab world and elsewhere in the world. It is such mediation that could forestall another Arab Spring.

BIBLIOGRAPHY

BOOKS

Aguilera, Donna C. *Crisis Intervention: Theory and Methodology*. 8th ed. New York: Mosby, 1998.

Beer, Jennifer E. with Eileen Steif. *The Mediator's Handbook*. Canada: New Society Publishers, 1997.

Bercovitch, Jacob. *Studies in International Mediation*, Palgrave Macmillan, New York 2003.

Carnegie, Dale. *How to Win Friends and Influence People*. Pocket Books, 1981

Chan, Henry A. *The Humanity of Mediators: From A Study of the Major Concepts of Viktor E. Frankl*. Lima, Ohio: Wyndham Hall Press, 2007.

Ehusani, George, *An Afro-Christian Vision "OZOVEHE!" Toward A More Humanized World*. (New York: University Press of America, 1991).

Frankl, Viktor E., *The Will to Meaning:Foundations and Applications of Logotherapy*, New York, Meridian Press, 1988.

Griffee, Dale T., *Research Tips: Interview Data Collection*, Journal of Developmental Education, National Center for Developmental Education, Appalachian State University, Boone, NC, 2005, p. 36

Gelvin, James L. *The Arab Uprisings*, what everyone needs to know. Oxford University Press. 2012

Hart, Michael. *The 100: A Ranking of the Most Influential Persons in History*. Citadel Press, 1992.

Hoffman, Bruce. *Inside Terrorism*. Columbia University Press, 2006

Hope, Mary Kendall. Iraq: *How Conflict Resolution Can Defeat Terrorism.* Eloquent Books (2008).

Hugh, Miall, *Conflict Transformation: A Multi-Dimensional Task, Berghof Handbook for Conflict Transformation*, 2004.

Juhasz, Antonia. *The Bush Agenda: Invading the World, One Economy at a Time.* HarperCollins Publishers, Inc. New York, 2006.

Nwachukwu, Anthony. Keeping Human Relationships Together: *Self Guide to Healthy Living [Studies in Spiritual Psychology vis-à-vis Human Values*]. Bloomington, *iUniverse Publishers*, 2010.

Sisk, D. Timothy. *Power sharing and international mediation in ethnic conflicts.* Carnegie Corp of NY. (1996).

Tylor, Edward B. *Primitive Culture*, 1871.

Ury, William. *Getting Past No: Negotiating with Difficult People.* (1991) New York: Random House.

Ury, et al. *Getting to Yes: Negotiating Agreements without Giving In* (1991) New York: Penguin Books.

ARTICLES, JOURNALS, ENCYCLOPEDIAS AND INTERNET SOURCES

A&E Television Networks, 2012

(ajami Fouad. *http://www.foreignaffairs.com/articles/137053/fouad-ajami/the-arab-spring-at-one*. Retrieved April 22, 2012).

Arthur Schechter. *www.Schechtergroup.com*. Retrieved 04/19/12)

http://middleeast.about.com/od/yemen/p/ali-abdullah-saleh-profile.htm. Retrieved March 12, 2012.

http://history1900s.about.com/od/saddamhussein/p/saddamhussein.htm. Retrieved April 12, 2012

http://atheism.about.com/od/popejohnpaulii/a/iraqwar.htm. Retrieved May 1, 2012.

"African Culture" (AMHARA) accessed on February 5, 2011 from africaguide.com (2010)

AmericanCatholic.org.

café-Syria.com

Collins English Dictionary–Complete & Unabridged 10th Edition, 2009.

http://www.commondreams.org/headlines03/0321-02.htm. (Retrieved May 1, 2012).

"Conflict Management", (Conflict) Work911/Bacal & Associates Business & Management Supersite, accessed on February 05, 2011 from http://www.work911.com/conflict/index.htm, 2010.

Conflict Research Consortium, University of Colorado. (Accessed 12/2011).

David Stout, *The New York Times*, August 31, 2006

http://www.differencebetween.net/miscellaneous/difference-between-religion-and-spirituality (Retrieved April 29. 2012).

Conjecture Corporation, 2012.

Cultural Empathy (Empathize) accessed on 30 January 2011 from EmpatiaResolutions.com (2008).

"Definition of Culture", (Culture) accessed on 30 January 2011 from Roshan Cultural Heritage Institute (2001)

Eastern European, (Europe) *InternationalBusinessCenter.org,* (2007), accessed on February 5, 2011 from Mediate.com, 2010.

"Empathy in Mediation", *(*Empathy) accessed on 30 January 2011 from faculty.mc3.edu.

Encyclopedia of World Biography. 2005-2006

Encyclopedia of Mental Disorders

Faure and Zartman *Negotiating with Terrorists,* Strategy, Tactics, and Politics, 2010

http://www.foreignaffairs.com/author/jack-a-goldstone; Mar/Apr. 2012, Vol. 91 Issue 2.

Heidi Blake (ed). *The Telegraph,* 2011

Iran Chamber Society, 2011

http://www.ivythesis.com/samples/ThesisPaperMethodo logy.htm.

http://www.jewishvirtuallibrary.org/jsource/biography/ Mubarak.html. Retrieved March 12, 2012).

Larry Johnson, *noquarterusa.net/arab-spring-or-middle-east-firestorm/.* Retrieved April 5, 2012).

Mahmoud Ahmadinejad. (2012). http://www.biography.com/ people/mahmoud-ahmadinejad-38656. (Retrieved 02:47, Jul 07, 2012).

Marc Lynch. *http//thebrowser.com/intervies/marc-lynch-on-Origins-of-the-Arab-Uprising*. Retrieved April 21, 2012).

Merriam-Webster's Dictionary of Law, 1996

mw1.meriam-webster.com

Oregon Mediation Center, Inc. 2011

http://www.philosophyofreligion.info/whos-who/historic-figures/st-thomas-aquinas/ (Retrieved 07/21/2012).

Rahim, M. A. (2002) Toward a theory of managing organizational conflict. The International Journal of Conflict Management, 13, 208.

rbenjamin.com. (Accessed 12/11/2011).

religion. (n.d.). *Dictionary.com Unabridged.* Retrieved July 17, 2012, from Dictionary.com website: http://dictionary.reference.com/browse/religion

Richelson, (ed.) *National Security Archive.* 2011

Robinson., *Ontario Consultants on Religious Tolerance,* 2011

Sgubini, Alessandra. Mediation and Culture: How different cultural backgrounds can affect the way people negotiate and resolve disputes. Mediate.com. 2011.

Suzanne Goldenberg (ed). *The Guardian*, 2011

The *Department of Veterans Affairs, Office Of The Dispute Resolution Specialist* (Accessed 12/11/2011).

The Harvard Negotiation Project (Accessed 01/12/2012)

The New Jerusalem Bible

The New York Times Company, 2006

The President and Fellows of Harvard College (2010).

The U.S. and the Middle East Since 1945, A Guide to Mideast Policy from Harry Truman to George W. Bush. http//About.com/middleeast. Retrieved 04/19/12.)

William, Saletan, The Slate Group, a Division of the Washington Post Company. http://www.slate.com/articles/technology/future_tense/2011/07/springtime_for_twitter.html

Zumeta, Zena, *Styles Of Mediation* Mediate.com. (2000).